The American Revolution in the West

George Rogers Clark portrait by James Burton Longacre, an idealization not done during Clark's lifetime.
Courtesy of the National Portrait Gallery, Smithsonian Institution, Washington, D.C.

The American Revolution in the West

George M. Waller

Nelson-Hall Chicago

Library of Congress Cataloging in Publication Data

Waller, George Macgregor, 1919-
    American Revolution in the West.

    Includes index.
    1.   Northwest, Old—History—
Revolution, 1775-1783.   2.   Clark, George
Rogers, 1752-1818.   3.   Indians of North
America—Wars—1775-1783.
I.   Title.   E263.N84W32   973.3'0977
75- 44471
ISBN 0-88229-279-X

Manufactured in the United States of America

To my wife
Martha

Contents

List of Illustrations

List of Maps

Cartography by Robert Lewis Blake

Acknowledgments

One of the pleasures of authorship lies in recollecting those who have helped. From the beginning the enthusiastic encouragement of my associates on the Indiana American Revolution Bicentennial Commission was highly gratifying. Among them were the first chairman, former Governor Roger D. Branigin; his successor, Walter Helmke; former director James M. Guthrie; and a assistant director Dale E. Fruchtnicht; Lieutenant Governor Robert D. Orr; Secretary of State Larry A. Conrad; Hubert H. Hawkins, director of the Indiana Historical Bureau; Carl H. Armstrong, director of the Indiana State Museum and Division of Museums and Memorials; Richard A. Greene; and William Lloyd, assistant to the governor.

Dr. Donald F. Carmoney of Indiana University, also on the Commission, gave the manuscript a careful reading and the benefit of his comments, as did my colleagues at Butler University, Dr. Emma Lou Thronbrough and Dr. George W. Geib; Gayle Thornbrough, editor of the Indiana Historical Society; Jon B. Turpin, Indiana Junior History Society; and Dr. Susan Reed Stifler.

The cooperation and stimulating consultations with Mrs. James E. Noland, Mrs. Howard R. Meeker, Jr., and Mrs. George T. Finney of the Indiana Museum Society and the Indiana State Museum have been valuable. So has help provided by Robert L. Lagemann, Superintendent of the George Rogers Clark National Historic Park; Howard H. Peckham, Director of the William L. Clements Library at the University of Michigan; Christine Schelshorn, Archivist of the State Historical Society of Wisconsin; Patricia B. Reibel, Fort Pitt Museum; Ann R. Mannarino, Mead Art Gallery, Amherst College; Dr. Jackson I. Cope, University of Southern California; and Robert Stalcup, Butler University.

In Vincennes, Indiana, Thomas S. Emision and Thomas Krasean of the Old Northwest Bicentennial; Mrs. H. W. Ramsey, Vincennes Historical Society; and Miss Maxine Batman, Vincennes Public Library, offered suggestions and assistance.

My office assistants at Butler University, Tom Dyer, Thomas Freas, Gregory Gossard, William Groth, Jennifer and Craig Lowry, Edward Lutz, Edward Shacklee, James Sharp, Andrew Sheff, and Waynes Sturtevant have spared me many details and given loyal support.

My wife, Dr. Martha S. Waller, read the drafts with care and insight despite her own heavy professional and domestic obligations and cheerfully bore my preoccupations and absences incident to an author's task. To her the volume is dedicated, with love.

Preface

Despite the fact that the center of population in the United States is in the Middle West, most of the events and historical treatments of the American Revolution have been related to the struggle for independence in the original thirteen states along the Eastern seaboard. The people in a seven-or eight-state area stretching from western Pennsylvania to the Mississippi River will not find their own regions represented in most histories of two hundred years ago. Yet this region had an important and exciting part in the American Revolutionary War.

This is a narrative history of the American Revolutionary War in the West, a story largely neglected or touched upon so briefly that its compelling narrative is lost, its relevance for the larger war unnoticed. The book is intended for the general reader who wants to know the story of those men and women who fought to defend their homesteads in the new frontier and to open the lands beyond the Ohio to eventual American settlement. It is meant for those who seek the revolutionary heritage of their own region, whose interest in the war has been aroused by the Bicentennial, and for the many who just like to read history. It should be valuable for the interested high school and college history students as well. Perhaps it should be considered important for those in other parts of the country who may be unaware of the war that took place far from the marching armies of George Washington.

At any rate, it presents with comparative brevity an account that cannot be found elsewhere, yet with sufficient detail to follow the ebb and flow of the struggle, vignettes of heroism, and with a full account of the major triumphs and defeats. It avoids the literary flourishes of overly romantic writers, the academic profundities of scholarly works, and the lengthy detail of biographers who have written of one or another of the West's leaders. Based on an extensive reading of the original sources, the work seeks to present an accurate account with clarity, bringing order to a much confused subject, while yet not sacrificing colorful or meaningful detail.

At the heart of the story is the remarkable young man, George Rogers Clark. Many people confuse him with his youngest brother, William, the Clark of the Lewis and Clark Expedition in 1805. Yet George Rogers Clark was not only America's outstanding leader in the West during the Revolution but also a major figure in the Revolutionary War as a whole. Indeed, he was a man often compared to George Washington. Like Washington, he suffered the trials and frustrations of fighting without enough men, money, and equipment, whether engaged in defending the Kentucky outposts or attempting offensive measures against the British in the Northwest. His generalship, like Washington's, owed most to his consummate qualities of leadership. And, like Washington's, his contribution to the fledgling United States cannot be minimized. He established the basis for realistic claims to an area larger than all the original thirteen states, the lands west of the Appalachians to the Mississippi, successfully won by the Republic's peacemakers at Paris.

Clark is seen against the backdrop of a war on the frontier that emerges as a small classic of endurance and daring, horror and suffering, vision and malice. It was a long and wearying struggle, the longest war America has ever fought except for the conflict in Vietnam. In the West, it encompassed four areas. This account traces parallel events involving the defense of the Kentucky stations, the weak and frustrated Regulars in the garrisons of the Upper Ohio, the struggles against Indians and British Loyalists in the inner settlements scattered in the western valleys of the Appalachians, and the westward thrusts to the Wabash and Mississippi along with the thin wedge of settlement that reached west in Tennessee to the Great Bend of the Cumberland. Though seen only as adversaries, the Indian tribes and their British leaders are put in a perspective that clarifies the problem of tribal locations, strength, and effectiveness.

The book's narrative conveys the courage, frustration, and suffering of the times without the need for hyperbole. That it was an Indian war that started long before the Declaration of Independence and continued long after peace treaties were signed is made evident, as well as the fact that Virginians played the major parts in the war in the West. As in other regions of the Revolutionary conflict, the war here saw inner conflict, too, between rival interest groups, military commands, and leading personalities. The frontiersman is not glorified. Many of them were guilty of cruelties that brought retaliation from Indians who might otherwise have stood aside.

No other book tells the story of the war in the West. A number of very old biographies of George Rogers Clark, of which James A. James's is the most reliable, are no longer easily obtained. They are lengthy, often uncritical in their acceptance of local traditions, confused in organization, and lacking in modern interpretations. Insofar as they go outside the details of Clark's life these accounts are misleading in their random selectivity and lack clarity in presenting the course of events. More recent Clark biographies are also out of print, except for a reprint edition of John Bakeless, and are riddled with errors of fact and dubious interpretations. Articles on Clark in *American Heritage,* December, 1973, October, 1962, are full of errors. All are marked by imaginary constructs of conversations and flamboyant romanticizing.

Local histories are hard to find, often antiquarian in tone, and treat of aspects of the war only in their own areas. A recent work, Jack M. Sosin's *The Revolutionary Frontier 1763-1783* (Holt, Rinehart, Winston, 1967), treats of the war in the quadrangle between the Great Lakes, the Mississippi, and the mouth of the Ohio in parts of two chapters.

Introduction

Brave Lewis our colonel an officer bold,
At the mouth of Kanawha did the Shawnees behold,
On the tenth of October at the rising sun
The armies did meet and the battle begun.

One thousand one hundred we had on Ohio,
Two thirds of this number to the battle did go,
The Shawnees nine hundred, some say many more,
We formed our battle on the Ohio shore.*

These couplets begin an epic existing in several variations in which some unknown versifiers celebrated the Battle of Point Pleasant in 1774. This fight was the first major clash between Indians and advancing white frontiersmen in the Ohio Valley since the British had defeated the Great Lakes tribes over ten years before to end Pontiac's Conspiracy. It signaled the beginning of long years of warfare as Americans pushed the frontier from the Appalachians to the Ohio River and beyond to the Mississippi.

The encounter at Point Pleasant on the banks of the Kanawha and Ohio rivers was the only real battle of the brief Lord Dunmore's War in the fall of 1774. John Murray, Lord Dunmore, was the last royal governor of Virginia under the British. Becoming interested in western land, he had ordered Fort Pitt repaired and reoccupied, realizing that its position, where the Allegheny and Monongahela meet to form the Ohio River, was the key to white settlement of land on both sides of the Ohio. The Shawnee, alarmed at this threat to their territory as well as by that posed by surveyors and

---

*R.C. Thwaites and Louis P. Kellogg, *Documentary History of Dunmore's War, 1774* (Madison, Wis.: Wisconsin Historical Society, 1905), p. 433.

settlers moving down the Ohio and into their hunting grounds in Kentucky, sought an alliance with their neighbors, the Delaware and the Mingo, and with the Cherokee farther south.

Dunmore's agent at Fort Pitt, Dr. John Connally, aroused the governor by reports of impending Indian warfare. Hardly needing any urging, Dunmore launched his war in anticipation of attack, despite the fact that reliable reports indicated that the Indians were willing to keep the peace. The Shawnee, unsuccessful in gathering allies from other tribes, had to fight alone and outnumbered.

At Point Pleasant, the warriors met forces led by Colonel Andrew Lewis, who had moved down the Kanawha River with men from the inner settlements in the Greenbrier Valley and the tributaries of the upper Tennessee River. After a day-long struggle, the Indians withdrew north of the Ohio, suffering few losses but leaving Lewis with heavy casualties. Notwithstanding this setback, Lewis advanced to meet a column under Lord Dunmore himself coming down the Ohio. The two forces joined and converged on the Shawnee camps clustered along the Scioto. The outnumbered Indians were compelled to sign a temporary agreement to permit white settlement south of the Ohio.

Marching with Dunmore was twenty-two-year-old George Rogers Clark, holding a captain's commission signed by the governor. The young man, destined to become America's most prominent leader in the West during the Revolutionary War, found himself companion-in-arms with many of the men who would serve with him through that war, fighting under a new flag, against the flag they now followed. Their names, John Gibson, James Robertson, Matthew Arbuckle, William Harrod, Joseph Bowman, Leonard Helm, Simon Kenton, deserve an honored place, along with Clark's, in the hearts of Americans who commemorate the struggle to win the West for the new United States.

Within two years, the struggle with the Indians revived by Lord Dunmore's War took on new seriousness with the outbreak of the American Revolution. In the West it was mainly an Indian war, but with a difference because the tribes were British-led and British-supplied. British Regulars, at Detroit and scattered in several other posts around the Great Lakes, were too few to mount a major attack against American settlements. Great Britain was counting on the thousands of Indians who lived in the lands between the Great Lakes, the Ohio, and the Mississippi to take up the hatchet against frontier fighters of the United States. The British were ready to furnish leadership and ample supplies.

Tribes once loyal to the French explorers and traders who first penetrated the mid-section of America had transferred their friendship grudgingly though not entirely to the British after France lost Canada in 1763. The Indians offered little resistance to British fur traders and soldiers who came west. After all, the tribesmen set great store by the cloth, kettles, knives, paint, guns, ammunition, and hundreds of other articles they could obtain in trade. But towards white men who came west to make their homes the Indians' attitude was very different. As the colonies expanded they had been pushed ever farther westward. As prospective settlers came through the valleys of the Appalachians into the West, Indians grimly set themselves against these men who felled the forests, slaughtered the game, and raised their cabins. To stop this threat, many warriors would be inclined to accept the support offered by British authorities. From the ranks of Indians already hostile to the settlers, the British would hope for enough fighting men to hold the West for the Crown.

The war in the West was not only an Indian war; it was also largely Virginia's war. It was fought over lands claimed by that state, principally by men whose loyalties lay with Virginia. There were settlers from Pennsylvania on the upper Ohio and in the southwest frontiersmen from North Carolina lived in the valleys of the Holston, Watauga, Nolichucky, and upper Tennessee rivers. Indeed, the whole frontier drew families from many states. But Virginians predominated, fighting with special devotion for a cause they believed was uniquely theirs.

The British and their Indians were not the only enemy. During the Revolution, Virginia was fighting in the West against rival Pennsylvania interests. We may interpret military strategy as being devised not merely to fight the British but also to forestall Pennsylvania claims to lands Virginia hoped to settle. Further, frontier leaders had to deal with an influx of unpatriotic land-grabbers, with Loyalists who sided with the British, and with a considerable number of men who wanted the entire region made independent of Virginia. It was a war in which personal rivalries and the jealousies between militiamen and soldiers of the Regular army frequently obstructed plans to fight the Indians or the

British. On top of all this, Americans became aware that their wartime ally, France, was showing signs of willingness to let the West remain British or yielding to Spanish designs on it. Preoccupation with these problems sometimes almost obscured the realities of Indian warfare on the frontier.

The western war ebbed and flowed in four regions from Kittanning on the Allegheny above Pittsburgh to the mouth of the Ohio. One theater of the war was the area of the upper Ohio, defended by a garrison of Regulars at Fort Pitt. This garrison controlled posts north along the Allegheny and south along the Ohio as far as the Kanawha River. Next, at the western base of the Appalachians were the inner frontier settlements on the Greenbrier and along New River. Another inner frontier farther south was made up of settlers on the Holston, Clinch, Watauga, and Nolichucky rivers, a frontier that after 1780 penetrated westward to the new stations on the Cumberland around what is now Nashville, Tennessee. Finally, projecting west to the Ohio River lay the Kentucky stations. During the war they thrust their influence to the French villages on the Mississippi and the Wabash (the Illinois country as it was called), and to the mouth of the Ohio.

The American Revolution in the West produced no major campaigns utilizing large-scale forces. It was a wearying war of guerilla tactics, most successful for either side when they moved small forces swiftly against unsuspecting targets. The problems of equipping, feeding, and transporting large numbers of men in wilderness conditions could not be overcome. Consistent military efforts failed for lack of men, money, or supplies. Distance and rugged terrain imposed insuperable obstacles for all sizable expeditions.

But for gallantry and courage as well as for sheer concentrated horror and suffering, for hardihood and vision as well as for savagery, malice, and frustration, the story of the war in the West is equal to that of the larger war in the East. Men too few, supplies scarce, money lacking were problems the nation faced on both fronts. Before launching into it, let us first note the general origins of the war and the particular views frontiersmen had about it.

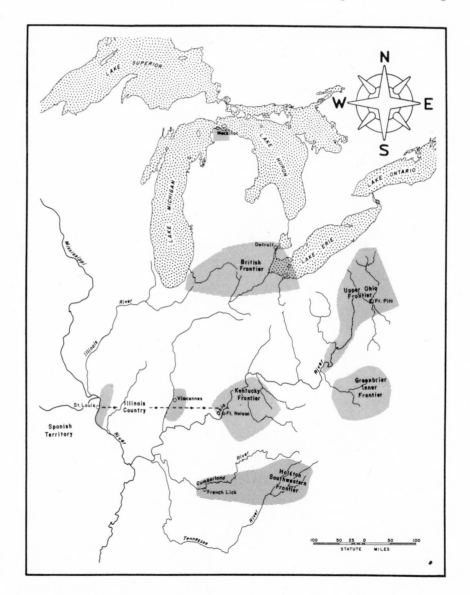

Frontiers of the War in the West.

One

Thirteen Clocks Striking Together

The principles of the American Revolution may be said to have been as various as the thirteen states that went through it, and in some sense almost as diversified as the individuals who acted in it."*

The causes for the American Revolution are complex. To understand how the colonies moved to the final step of declaring independence is not easy. Numerous and varied, the purposes of the people who opposed Britain were sometimes contradictory and even buried in their subconscious minds, spoken in slogans and catchwords that may have meant both more and less than they expressed. No wonder it has been difficult for historians to agree on the importance of different issues in the struggle with Great Britain.

It may well be that those Americans who rallied to the cause of independence listened less to the legalistic or logical arguments of leaders like John Adams or Thomas Jefferson than to anxieties and fears produced in their own minds and hearts by the disordered conditions of the time. Anger, enthusiasm, feverish language, and intensity of passion directed against both local authorities and the British government may explain American behavior better than a sober list of clearly calculated grievances.

The colonies before 1763 had been part of a weak British imperial system; the policies of that government, constantly changed and erratically applied, created a sense of instability and nagging fears of what might come next. Such suspicion affected the colonists in America more than the actual regulations themselves. In addition, during the preceding century almost every colony had experienced

---

*John Adams, quoted in Merrill Jensen, *The Founding of a Nation* (New York: Oxford University Press, 1968), p. xii.

changes that produced internal tensions and social strains. These stresses were not enough to cause a revolution. Going back many years and stemming from both British policy and American conditions, they provided an underlying sensitivity and irritability that make the vigorous reactions to British actions between 1763 and 1776 more understandable.

The British victory over France in 1763 added a new factor to the colonists' uneasiness. The outcome of the Great War for Empire, known as the French and Indian War (1754-1763) in America, left the colonists exhilarated by the conquest of Canada. After years of intercolonial jealousy, they emerged from the war more unified and with an enlarged sense of self-importance. Exaggerating their own contributions to the victory, they felt liberated, if only psychologically.

This was a poor time for Great Britain to impose either new or tighter restrictions on Americans. Elimination of French power in Canada removed much of the colonists' need for the mother country's protection. Yet British authorities kept the Redcoats in America in numbers unprecedented for peacetime. It could not have escaped the notice of the leaders in London that keeping royal troops in America would strengthen their hand in enforcing government regulations. It is no wonder that the Redcoats came to be a symbol of British oppression in American minds.

The timing of the application of new regulations on the colonies was as essential in the British view as it was unfortunate from the viewpoint of Americans. The colonial system of regulation, developed in the last half of the seven-teenth century and the first part of the eighteenth, had not been consistently enforced. Lax administration, distance, and the colonists' exercise of increasing responsibility for their own government had made the system tolerable, even beneficial, to the colonies. However much such a live-and-let-live policy may have suited Americans, Britain by the mid-eighteenth century was already encountering problems. Many small, hardly noticed changes were creating distrust in some groups in America.

With the end of the war in 1763, the need for a general overhaul of the colonial system became urgent. The British treasury was low, taxes on the English landed gentry high. A vast new area of America taken from France had to be provided with a system of government and defense. The demands of colonists for lands west of the Appalachians required policies of land allotment and provisions for avoiding Indian hostilities. The latter problem was almost immediately underlined by the Indian uprising called Pontiac's Conspiracy, in 1763.

The laws regulating trade seemed to require stricter enforcement to maintain a profitable flow of commerce. A more reliable collection of customs duties was needed to meet the cost of administering the system. It seemed reasonable to ask the colonists to bear taxes to maintain regiments stationed in the colonies for their own defense. Colonial courts and currency systems were expected to work towards the prosperity of the Empire and to the advantage of British merchants.

If the actions which followed—taxation without

representation and harassment of trade—seemed to Americans like an end to their liberties, many British leaders simply could not understand why. They denied any intention of passing laws that did not conform to colonial needs. They also refused to recognize the rights that the Americans claimed. To some in England it seemed that Americans were confusing privileges with rights. And admittedly, many British legislators voted for measures that America would oppose without knowing nor caring what mere colonists might think. When an uproar followed in the towns and villages of these far-off lands, members of Parliament often became convinced that it proved the weakening of the traditional allegiance, giving all the more reason to make clear Parliament's right to rule.

It is no use blaming King George III. The young monarch was not intentionally a tyrant, as some Americans declared. He was an earnest though inexperienced politician, as yet unable to control the government or to find the men who might solve its problems. Parliament was divided into many political factions, self-centered in their concerns for their own political futures, personal ambitions, social and economic interests. Certainly they were insensitive to the American viewpoint, unconcerned except to follow the measures of their own particular parliamentary leaders.

§ Britain Tightens Control

The acts of George Grenville, prime minister between 1763 and 1765, were largely undertaken on his own initiative and passed blindly by his followers in Parliament. The Proclamation of 1763 temporarily closed to settlement lands west of a line along the Appalachian watershed. A modified Molasses Act followed by the Sugar Act changed a number of trade regulations. A Quartering Act required colonial governments to provide supplies and shelter for British troops. The Currency Act prohibited the issue of paper money in the colonies and the use of depreciated colonial currency in settling debts.

Overshadowing these other regulations, the Stamp Act provoked the greatest outburst in the colonies. The act called for the purchase of stamps for all legal and commercial documents, liquor licenses, newspapers and other printing, playing cards, and dice. The revenue raised was to help defray the costs of colonial government.

Vigorous protest came from the delegates of nine colonies who met in the Stamp Act Congress in New York. More significantly, there was organized resistance to the purchase of the stamps, along with mobs, riots, and some refusal to trade with Britain. These developments resulted in Grenville's fall from power, the repeal of the Stamp Act, and modification of some of the customs duties and tariffs. But Parliament continued to declare its right to tax the colonies.

In 1767, Charles Townshend, an officer in a new ministry, made another effort to solve Britain's severe financial problems with new legislation, imposing duties on a number of items and tightening enforcement of the laws governing trade. Again colonial opposition was aroused, and again colonial resistance was a major reason for repeal of most of the new duties.

These events brought the festering discontents of many groups with different grievances to a head. Adroit leaders like Samuel Adams and Thomas Paine, through speeches, pamphlets, letters, and newspapers, helped to unite those groups with separate complaints into a body holding common grievances aimed against a particular target, the British government. In this way diverse groups were able to join together to make a revolution, though each group may have been seeking relief from things that did not trouble the others.

Although most of the unpopular colonial measures had been repealed by 1770, there remained a nucleus of aroused and apprehensive Americans, now more sensitive than ever to possible British interference with their trade and especially their presumed rights of self-government. Among these Americans, only a few looked forward to independence or plotted to exploit British actions in order to win followers. These extremists were unrepresentative of the mass of Americans who, with their leaders, hoped for accommodation with Great Britain.

In 1773, the ministry of Lord North at the head of a group called "the King's Friends" again gave revolutionary leaders in America a chance to arouse the people. North put through an act giving the British East India Company a monopoly on the tea trade in America. He probably did not anticipate serious American reaction, but after resulting acts of lawlessness like the Boston Tea Party and other violent protests, he took strict punitive measures against a number of colonies. His overreaction set the stage for the final acts of resistance that led to the decision to break away from British rule.

§ **Aroused Colonists Seek Independence**

In their opposition to Great Britain, Americans disagreed about methods. In many areas local issues divided people so much that sometimes they lost sight of their grievances against Britain. As their protests and passions interacted they produced independence and war, unforeseen and unwanted by many. Perhaps people acted, as they still do, without being completely aware of their motives. Altogether their grievances may not have added up to enough to drive them to join an independence movement. Economic pressures may have been insufficient to account for their radical slogans. It may even be argued that essential freedoms were not substantially threatened by any of the new British actions.

Some, ultimately most of those who rebelled, had long suspected a conspiracy to deprive Americans of their liberties. They protested and marched because British policies seemed to them to invade their principles or rights. Others, fewer and with special interests at stake, fought against measures and policies that threatened their profits or were in conflict with their trade.

Colonial leaders were themselves divided over how much authority they should wield and how much they should take from Britain. There was also a further question of who among the various groups should furnish leadership. In many colonies the country people tended to be at odds with the representatives of the towns. Frontiersmen might think themselves disregarded by the ruling gentry of the eastern seacoast. Ordinary people, in some instances, resented the power of wealthy merchants and the plantation aristocracy. Though such problems were local, people would join together against the king if they believed that the objects of their discontent were supported by the power of the British government or that they might gain their ends during a wholesale change such as a revolution.

So the leaders in each colony had to appeal to a wide variety of divided colonists who had actual grievances or only vague discontents, and who were suspicious of their own rulers, of each other, and of the British. Certain of those men, foremost in the mounting opposition to British regulation, may have based their protests on their own economic well-being and property rights, using demagogic tricks to arouse the common people to their support. It may have appeared to some of these ordinary people that their leaders intended to "keep one foot on the lower classes while they kicked the British with the other," as historian Edmund Morgan has put it. Once aroused, ordinary townspeople and farmers would begin to see the chance to put forward their own complaints. Many historians believe that the efforts of these common people before and during the war and in the formation of new states amounted to an attempt at an "inner" or social revolution along with the War for Independence.

Men like John Adams, George Washington, Thomas Jefferson, or Benjamin Franklin were certainly neither sel-

fish and narrow-minded nor the dupes of agitators. They took seriously the political rights they believed were embodied in their English heritage and long supported in the actions of their colonial legislatures. It did not escape them that Parliament, dominated by local interests and petty ambitions, was passing ill-considered and hasty acts which affected America in a way that indicated British politicians did not know how to run an empire.

American leaders really believed in the charges they hurled—charges that seem fanatical, hypocritical, or propagandistic—accusations of "conspiracy," "corruption," "tyranny," "slavery." These terms covered any and all discontents, real or imagined. They came to mean even more than they seemed to, arousing passions, leading people into directions not consciously desired, towards goals not originally anticipated.

For the shapers of the American Revolution we may conclude that the movement for separation from Britain came finally with reluctance. It resulted from a political struggle over power and its use, which in turn reflected the separation of social and economic concerns held by those on this side of the ocean from those in the mother country. The Revolutionary movement finally took form as a question of legal and ideological principles on which the two sides disagreed. The issue came down to opposition to Parliament's authority to govern the colonies rather than what kind of taxes were levied or what regulations passed or whether or not some groups were hurt by them.

As the crisis mounted, the king's decision to use

coercion against American resisters forced Americans to choose. They must submit, or fight for privileges and rights they believed they already possessed—that, indeed, they had long enjoyed. Many did submit out of loyalty to the Crown and appreciation for the benefits that the imperial connection gave them. Those in the Continental Congress who laid it on the line by signing the Declaration of Independence, with those who supported them, embarked on a long and dangerous course to win a new, independent United States. To unite the colonies in a movement for independence was, as John Adams pointed out, " . . . a singular example in the history of mankind. Thirteen clocks were made to strike together. . . ."*

---

*Letter to Niles, Feb. 13, 1818. *The Works of John Adams*, 10 vols., ed. C. F. Adams (Boston, 1850-1856), 10:283.

Two

The Mind and Heart of the West

"The Revolution was in the minds and hearts of the people . . . before hostilities commenced."*

On the western borders of the colonies, the issues that had aroused the seaboard towns and the back country east of the Appalachians were doubtless also matters of concern along with their own special interests. Surveyors and scouts for eastern land companies and the men appointed to deal with Indian problems generally reflected the views of those for whom they worked. But many families and individuals had probably come west to escape the riots, tensions, and quarreling in the East. Some certainly did not care to take part in the conflict and some remained loyal to Great Britain.

Whether families on the frontier supported the Revolution, stood neutral, or remained firm in their attachment to the Crown, depended on many factors. It is not clear that religion, social status, economic class, or occupation made any discernible difference. Often the choice was apparently a personal one. For many no real choice existed. Though they might have been happy to remain outside the conflict, the presssure of numbers around them for one side or the other might determine their part. Also, individual commitments might waver depending on the success or failure of military forces operating in their area. Where Crown officials were effective—governors, Indian superintendents, or other royal agents—large groups might resist the patriotic appeal, as many did in the western parts of the colonies below Virginia and in the western areas of Pennsylvania and New York.

§ **Western Frontier**

The West in the Revolutionary era was an area

---

*John Adams to Thomas McKean, Nov. 26, 1815. *Works*, ed. C. F. Adams, 10:180.

bounded on the north by the Great Lakes, by the Mississippi River on the west, and to the east and south by the Western Appalachians and the Ohio River Valley and tributary streams. Colonists had begun years before to move out to the headwaters of the Potomac, James, and other rivers of the Atlantic coastal plain. They had then moved into the mountain valleys between the Appalachian ridges, the Shenandoah, southwest into the valleys of the Greenbrier, Holston, Watauga, and Clinch rivers, and north along the Susquehanna and its tributaries.

By the time of the Revolution, scattered settlers were following the pathfinders and surveyors into new lands west of the mountains—the regions of the Allegheny and Monongahela rivers, down the Ohio toward the lush lands called Kentucky, and through the Cumberland Gap to either Kentucky or the settlements on the Cumberland.

Some avaricious explorers had their eyes on the Ohio country, north and west of the Ohio River, which was held by the Indians. Or they dreamed of the lands of the Illinois country, the region south of Lake Michigan along the Mississippi and the Wabash. French settlements remained at Detroit, Mackinac, and on the Wabash and Mississippi rivers from earlier years when Canada had belonged to France and its control had extended through this region. Since 1763 the French inhabitants had been joined by English traders, agents of the Crown, and military forces.

On the western side of the Mississippi River the Spanish held outposts from Saint Louis downriver to New Orleans, while the British had settled on the eastern bank at Natchez.

§ Virginia's Claims to the West

Most of the people on the western frontier came from North Carolina, Virginia, and Pennsylvania. Virginia's claim to the region was the most extensive, based on her original colonial grants. Since the war in the West was fought largely under the authority and direction of Virginia by frontiersmen, many of whom thought of themselves as Virginians, it is important to examine Virginia's attitudes towards the war.

The people of Virginia were among the most firmly united of all the colonies in their opposition to Great Britain. Theirs was the most settled colony with slight conscious divisions between social groups, little class antagonism or discontent with the aristocracy. Though social tensions were not obvious, the ruling group at Williamsburg was exhibiting a certain lack of confidence and signs of troubled spirits. They may have subconsciously blamed themselves for the pattern of idleness and luxury in their plantation life based on slave labor. Worry over unstable markets, restlessness over the debts that bound them to British merchants, and an awareness of the challenge of newer leaders heightened their feelings of unease.

Virginians on the frontier, looking back at their ruling group in the Tidewater, doubtless shared this uneasiness. If something was bothering them it was easier to blame it on the British than to try to understand their own problems. The British could be blamed for their fears, their sense of injury and oppression, even though these feelings stemmed in part from their own condition rather than British actions. At any rate, Virginia, more than any other area in the country, was almost unanimous in its determination to revolt.

Virginians on the frontier and in the settled regions were especially concerned by events between 1763 and 1774 involving that colony's western land claims. Virginia had long been expansionist. The prospects of profits from land and the need for new soil in which to cultivate tobacco had set leading men dreaming about the territory west of the mountains early in the century.

At first, victory over the French in 1763 had enhanced this prospect. Then Virginian land speculators had become alarmed at the activities of Pennsylvania traders also interested in western lands. The Pennsylvanians claimed land south of the Ohio River for their enterprise, the Grand Ohio Company, to which they attached men of importance from several colonies. The Company also enlisted powerful backing from leaders in British government and business. It proposed to settle a new colony, to be called Vandalia, in an area granted by the Iroquois at the Treaty of Fort Stanwix (1768), land which the Iroquois did not even occupy and which was, in fact, the territory of other Indian tribes.

This area, between the Appalachians and the Ohio, cut directly across the claims of the older Ohio Company of Virginia, made up of prominent Virginians, and lay within the boundaries claimed by Virginia. Fortunately for the governments of both Virginia and Pennsylvania, negotiations for the new colony bogged down in Britain, so that this project which would have taken western lands claimed by both colonies never succeeded. Speculators, including Pennsylvanians, Marylanders, and some Virginians, also failed to complete plans for private land claims that would have challenged Virginia's western interests when the Illinois Company and the Wabash Company failed.

Nor did Judge Richard Henderson from North Carolina succeed in making a new colony, Transylvania, out of the area between the Kentucky River and the Cumberland River, although he sent Daniel Boone to blaze the Wilderness Road from the Holston River settlements through the Cumberland Gap, and himself led a party of settlers to Boonesborough in the spring of 1775.

The failure of all these rivals to overturn Virginia's western claims before the outbreak of the Revolution increased long-held expectations for the colony's expansion, while it also aroused its competitive spirit. Prominent men interested in the lands north and west of the Ohio were also mightily cheered by the outcome of Lord Dunmore's War in the fall of 1774. Although to opponents of Virginia's western ambitions this war had been a thinly disguised use of force by speculators, unprovoked by any real Indian menace, Virginians themselves rejoiced in its outcome.

Actions of the British government promptly dashed

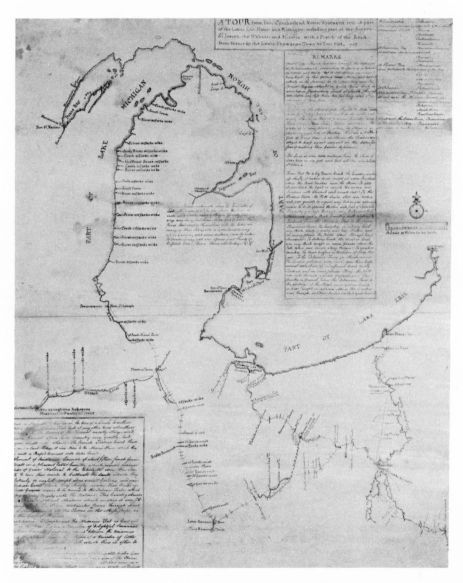

"Map of a Tour from Fort Cumberland. . . ," an unusually accurate early map of the West by Thomas Hutchins, 1762. The original is in the Henry E. Huntington Library.

Reproduced by permission of the Henry E. Huntington Library, San Marino, California.

the high hopes of land-hungry speculators. Dunmore's military gains were offset by news of Parliament's passage of the Quebec Act in the summer of 1774. This act put the land north and west of the Ohio River under the control of the governor of Canada while Virginia's interests in the area south and east of the river were still endangered by the pending Vandalia colony project. To Virginians, the Quebec Act seemed to support the Indians in their opposition to white expansion. The act promised the French inhabitants of the area security for their Roman Catholic faith, a religion suspect to many Americans. Moreover, it prohibited representative government and jury trials in that region, rights which American settlers would not forfeit. This British action presented Virginia with the threat that its borders would be cut off at the Appalachians.

Virginian expansionists regarded the Quebec Act as the last straw. Even Thomas Jefferson, who was not involved in land speculation, questioned the right of the British government to dispose of American land. He later made it one of the counts he leveled against George III in the Declaration of Independence.

§ Virginian George Rogers Clark

Because frontiersmen fought the war in the West largely by themselves, it is enlightening to learn how their most prominent leader, George Rogers Clark, understood the conflict. His attitude is particularly significant because in Virginia the back country and frontier leaders had few disagreements with the eastern gentry.

Clark, as well as the leaders at Williamsburg, had no doubt that Virginia's territory stretched west to the Mississippi from a point somewhere below the mouth of the Ohio in the south, almost to the southern end of the Great Lakes. Boundaries with Pennsylvania to the north and North Carolina on the south had not been run, but Virginia claimed an area embracing most of the present states of West Virginia, Ohio, Kentucky, Indiana, and Illinois, possibly even Michigan and Wisconsin, based on the boundaries of Virginia's colonial charter, in addition to the area of the parent state.

To Clark, the war in the West was important for the part it would play in overall military strategy in the Revolution, and also for the material gains victory would bring to him and his fellow Virginians. He stressed the strategic grounds of the war to Governor Patrick Henry and the state's new Revolutionary government. Instead of taking a defensive stand in the West, he advocated carrying the war to the enemy's country, eliminating those posts from which the British supplied the Indians and mustered them against Virginia's frontiers. Possession of the West would keep open the Ohio and Mississippi river channels by which Americans hoped to receive supplies from the Spanish in New Orleans. It would pin down British troops which might otherwise be used against Washington's forces in the East. There was the chance that Clark could win over the French in the villages along the Wabash and Mississippi. If he succeeded in this the western Indians, long loyal to the French who still maintained enormous influence over them, might be won. Clark thought, too, that activities in this area would deprive the

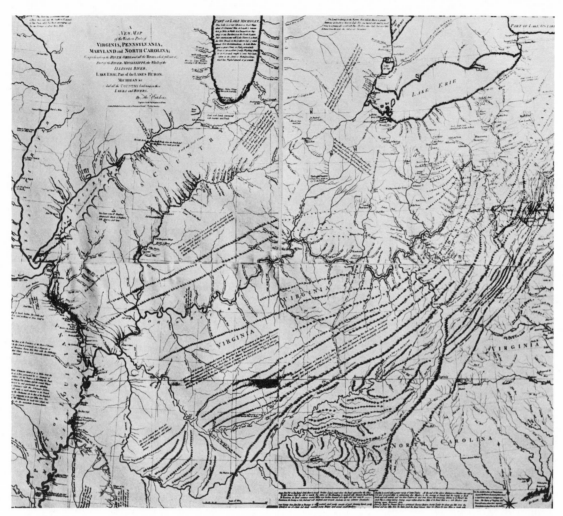

A New Map of the Western Parts of Virginia, Pennsylvania, Maryland, and North Carolina etc., published in London, November, 1778, by Thomas Hutchins. This is the only extensive map of the West contemporaneous with the Revolution. Hutchins had been a British Army engineer serving in the Ohio and Mississippi valleys from 1764 to 1772. New Jersey born, he refused to fight against the United States. He escaped imprisonment in England and joined the American army in the South in 1781. This map was published too late to serve Clark in his march to the Mississippi, but Clark and other American commanders in the West may have used Hutchins' preliminary sketches, maps, and descriptions which could have been available through friends of Hutchins, especially George Morgan, Indian agent for the United States at Pittsburgh.

British around the Great Lakes and in Canada of food products and furs which helped support them. In short, the best defense would be a good offense.

In addition to these strategic arguments, Clark and his supporters saw in the lands beyond Kentucky opportunities for personal wealth and public office. While the outbreak of the Revolution obliged them to defend the existing frontier, it also offered Virginia an opportunity to extend it. In addition, Virginia might forestall the schemes of North Carolinians and Pennsylvanians, not to mention the possible ambitions of the Spanish or French, if Britain should lose in the West.

Aglow with the possibilities, Clark wrote to his brother, "A richer and more beautiful country than this I believe has never been seen in America yet." He added that if their father once saw the area he would never rest until he owned land in it on which to live. With fellow Kentuckians in Harrodsburg, Clark petitioned the leaders of the Revolutionary movement in Virginia to defend the region. The frontiersmen promised to "support the present laudable cause" and "our common liberty." At first the Virginia Council rebuffed Clark's request for military stores. He dramatically admonished them, "If a country was not worth protecting it was not worth claiming." The Council saw the point and voted the required help.

In his discussions later with Indian leaders, Clark voiced complete agreement with the common notions about the war. Using simple phrases to tell the American story to the inquiring chiefs, he recounted that people had come to the New World to escape the oppression of the king. After letting them grow populous and prosperous, the king had ordered his governors to make the Americans pay tribute, "he did not care how much they took, so [long] as they left us enough to eat," and sent soldiers to make the Americans pay. In this way, "we got poor and was obliged to go naked, and at last we complained. The King got mad and made his soldiers kill some of our people. . . ."

For Virginia frontiersmen, then, loyalty to the new United States and justification for the Revolution arose from fear of British tyranny and belief in what they called British "corruption." Like their friends in the settled regions they did not doubt that they were fighting for what Jefferson so neatly phrased as, "life, liberty and the pursuit of happiness."

In addition the war in the West was a continuation of the conflict that had been mounting for several years between settlers, land prospectors, and traders on the one side and Indians on the other. The frontiersman's concern was protection from Indian attack. If he could not keep the Indians out of the struggle, if the Indians responded to the British call to arms, Virginia would have to strengthen its western defenses, strike back at the Indians, and attack the British outposts from which the Indians took their direction and support.

For many like Clark it was also a fight to win opportunities for wealth, land, and position in a new area so rich in promise. These attractions had been and continued to be the stuff of their dreams and imaginations. If successful, they hoped to make good their claim to a region reaching all the way to the Mississippi. If they failed, they might be driven back east of the Appalachians.

Success in the West might, moreover, win for all Americans an area vaster than that of the original thirteen states. Failure could mean a United States pinched into the Atlantic seaboard and ringed by the three great European powers of Britain, Spain, and France. It could even mean failure to establish independence. This heavy burden Virginia and her frontiersmen had to bear largely alone. The hard-pressed Continental armies of General Washington could spare little help.

The war in the West was destined to be a savage conflict against small British detachments and Indians whose antagonism had been aroused by preceding decades of white expansion. The brutal struggle involved fighting, murder, and retaliation on the part of both whites and Indians. It had been under way long before the Revolutionary War and was to continue long afterward.

Three

The Frontier Prepares

The War for American Independence began without a declaration of war. The fighting started when General Thomas Gage ordered British troops in Boston to seize radical leaders and military supplies at Concord. Lord North's ministry in London had determined that the colonists were in rebellion and resolved to suppress the movement by force if necessary. On 19 April, 1775, the Redcoats clashed with colonial militiamen gathered to oppose them at Lexington and Concord; the shots "heard 'round the world" were fired.

Not until more than a year later did representatives of the thirteen colonies sitting as the Second Continental Congress in Philadelphia gain enough unanimity of opinion to support the motion of Virginia's Richard Henry Lee, on 7 June, 1776, that "these united colonies are, and of right ought to be free and independent states." Even then divided delegates held back. A vote taken on 1 July showed New York, Pennsylvania, Delaware, and South Carolina still unwilling to commit themselves to independence.

When the Congress finally adopted the Declaration of Independence of 4 July, most colonies had already formed new state governments, in some cases, many months earlier. Civil war was raging between patriots and those loyal to Great Britain. Benedict Arnold and Ethan Allen had captured the British Fort Ticonderoga on the New England frontier more than a year before, although the subsequent attempt to take Quebec failed. The New England countryside had rallied to surround the British troops in Boston. These patriots fought the battle of Bunker Hill in June 1775. Congress had appointed George Washington to command the American army the following month, a year before the Declaration of Independence.

At first neither Congress nor the British wanted to use Indians in the war. Leaders on both sides well knew the appalling cruelty the tribes inflicted on their victims. The Indians generally avoided battles with organized forces, preferring to fall upon lightly defended frontier posts or cabins where they scalped, tortured, and murdered men, women, and children alike. In order to remain unencumbered, they took few captives and often tomahawked those they did drag off if the unhappy whites proved unequal to the march or angered their captors.

The Continental Congress decided in 1775 to attempt to keep the warriors neutral. Following British practice, Congress appointed commissioners of Indian affairs for the various colonial districts. Benjamin Franklin, Patrick Henry, and James Wilson were to serve for the middle department, comprising the frontiers of Pennsylvania, Virginia, and Maryland. In 1776 they appointed George Morgan, formerly a partner in the extensive trading firm of Baynton, Wharton, and Morgan, as their agent at Fort Pitt. In this way, direction of Indian affairs was centralized under the supervision of Congress rather than being left to the separate states and their sometimes contradictory policies.

But early in 1775, Massachusetts enlisted a few friendly Indians in active service. In retaliation, the British commander-in-chief, General Thomas Gage, ordered Governor Guy Carleton in Quebec and the British Indian superintendent in the southern district, John Stuart, to use Indians against the Americans on the frontiers. Although neither Carleton nor Stuart obeyed Gage's orders, the British were active in negotiating to keep the Indians from joining the Revolutionaries just as the American agents worked to win them to their cause. It was easy to mistake such efforts as attempts not only to deprive the enemy of Indian aid but to gain active Indian support as combatants. As a result of old grudges between the Indians and the settlers, the stronger tribes tended to side with British who were not, after all, after their land.

By 1776 George Washington advised Congress that the Indians were not likely to remain outside the struggle. Congress then authorized use of the Indians. But only where American forces dominated relatively weak tribes was there a likelihood that Indian allies might help fight the war for the frontiersmen. Although realizing the horrors of Indian warfare, American leaders came to agree with a western New Yorker who realistically observed, "that they may be better fighting for us than against us needs not argument." Unfortunately for the West, active Indian support on the American side was unlikely; at best American strength was only barely sufficient in some few areas to cow the Indians into uneasy neutrality.

A factor that influenced the British against utilizing Indians at first was the fear of endangering frontier families who were loyal to the Crown. Savage warfare was not apt to discriminate between patriots and Loyalists. During the first two years of the war, the British contemplated enlisting Indians as auxiliaries to their Regulars, so that the warriors could be kept under control. Despite British efforts, they could not restrain the Cherokee on the southern frontier.

§ Indian Unrest Grows

On the frontier, war came to the Southwest first. The nearest Cherokee towns were only about one hundred miles south and west of the settlements on the Holston, Watauga, and Nolichucky rivers. First were the Overhill Cherokee towns in the southwestern valleys of the Appalachians, particularly on the Little Tennessee River. South of them were the Middle Cherokee. Still farther south at the foot of the mountains, the Lower Cherokee lived on the Coosa, Etowa, Tugaloo and streams running into the Chattahoochee and Savannah rivers. To these Indians and to the Choctaw, Chickasaw, and Creek farthest south, John Stuart sent strict orders prohibiting indiscriminate attacks against the whites. At the same time, Stuart sent Isaac Thomas, a man active in Indian trade, to warn the Holston area that the Indians might not be restrained and to urge frontiersmen to accept land in West Florida under British protection. But many frontiersmen, even when they had Loyalist leanings, were unwilling to give up their lands to accept such an offer. Forced to defend themselves against Indian raids, they fought with the patriot militia despite their political attitudes.

The Overhill Cherokee were divided. Older leaders counseled restraint but the young warriors chafed at the loss of land given up in earlier treaties and the encroachment of restless, land-hungry frontiersmen beyond the lines of treaty agreements. British gifts, including thirty packhorse loads of ammunition to Dragging Canoe, the leader of the war party, served less to conciliate the Indians than to provide them with the means to fight.

White inhabitants in the region begged Stuart to hold off the Indians to give them time to move, protesting their loyalty to Britain. But at the same time they sent to the Virginia authorities for help and misrepresented Stuart's policy as one of inciting the Indians against them. Despite a strongly worded message Virginia directed to the Overhills to stay out of the conflict, Dragging Canoe prepared to attack. A visiting delegation of Iroquois, Delaware, and Shawnee from the north agreed, as did Tories operating among the Creeks farther south. John Stuart's brother Henry, along with another British agent, Alexander Cameron, managed to keep the Creek and Choctaw quiet so that the Cherokee had to fight alone.

In early July 1776, Dragging Canoe led three hundred warriors against the Holston outposts. The Raven of Chote attacked the whites at Carter's Valley with his forces, and Abram of Chilhowie struck the Wataugans. Three traders learned of the plans from an Indian woman married to another white trader. They warned John Sevier, one of the leaders of the region. Over three thousand gathered in their forts for protection, suffering from illness and confinement during that summer.

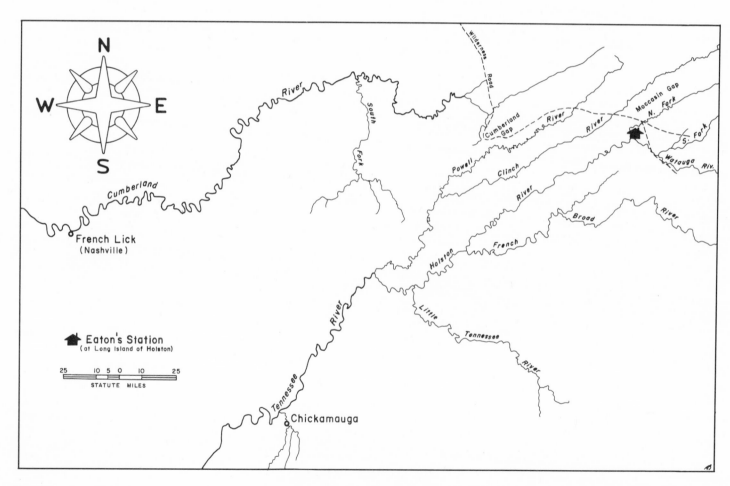

Southwestern Frontier

Five companies of militia defended Eaton's Station on the Holston and drove off the Indians under Dragging Canoe, who was wounded in the battle. James Robertson, commanding Fort Lee on the Watauga with John Sevier as his second-in-command, withstood a two weeks' siege by Chief Abram's forces, which finally withdrew just before a hundred Virginia militiamen arrived in relief. The Raven found the forts in Carter's Valley too strong.

Middle and Lower Cherokee raided along the Carolina and Georgia frontiers but were met by two hundred Georgians under Captain Samuel Jack at the Indians' Tugaloo River towns. General Griffith Rutherford of North Carolina went on to destroy the villages of the Middle and Lower Cherokee. Eleven hundred South Carolinians moved west under the command of Colonel Andrew Williamson and after a severe battle in which Williamson's aide, Colonel Hammond, displayed distinguished leadership, forced the Indians to flee. Colonel William Christian brought eighteen hundred troops from Virginia against the Overhill to end their threat.

By the spring of 1777, the Cherokee war on the frontier was over. The chiefs signed two treaties, one with South Carolina at Dewitt's Corner and one with Virginia and North Carolina at the Long Island of the Holston. Only the militant Dragging Canoe refused to desist. With his followers, he withdrew to Chickamauga Creek on the Tennessee River to form a new tribe, the Chickamauga. Except for the raids of this group later in the war, the defeated Cherokee provided only an occasional threat to the West during the following years. Other southern tribes remained lethargic or were used by the British against the Spanish settlements in West Florida.

§ **Expansion of the Frontier**

While the inhabitants of the Holston settlements were subduing the Cherokee, the frontier had already moved north and west of the Appalachians. People from east of the mountains had settled along the Ohio River as far down as the Scioto by 1773, coming from the Forks of the Ohio at Fort Pitt or cross-country from the Monongahela. Others had penetrated to the Greenbrier in the western valleys of the mountains. From there they could descend the Kanawha to the Ohio. At the end of March 1775, Daniel Boone led a path-making party from the Long Island of the Holston through Cumberland Gap northwest to the Kentucky River.

George Washington had traveled along the Ohio River to the Kanawha in the fall of 1770 to search out likely lands for himself, his relatives, and fellow veterans of the French and Indian War. Just as Washington was a surveyor in early life, so too was George Rogers Clark. Clark accompanied the party of a Reverend David Jones when he first canoed down the Ohio in the summer of 1772, sleeping at night on the gravel banks of the river. The next winter Clark settled on land south of Wheeling at the mouth of Grave Creek and worked with surveyors for military bounty lands in 1774 when he was not engaged in Lord Dunmore's War against the Shawnee.

In 1775 Clark was Hancock Lee's assistant in surveying lands on the North Elkhorn and Licking Rivers for William Crawford and the Ohio Company. The year before, John Floyd had been locating land throughout the Kentucky region for a number of Virginia leaders. Floyd settled St. Asaph's in May 1775. There, among some thirty settlers, were the prominent Virginia lawyers John Todd and Benjamin Logan, for whom the place was sometimes referred to as Logan's Fort. A year before, James Harrod with forty-some settlers had established Harrodstown, before vacating it upon rumors of Indian war. When Harrod returned in 1775 to find Harrodstown occupied by the McAfee brothers and their followers from Boonesborough, he moved a few miles south along the Salt River to start the settlement of Boiling Spring.

Richard Henderson led a party following Daniel Boone's axemen along the Wilderness Road to Boonesborough on the Kentucky River. There he sought to establish a new colony which he called Transylvania, shaped to his own grandiose schemes. Henderson, arriving on 20 April, 1775, found little encouragement from others already settling Kentucky. Frontiersmen were cool to Henderson's claim that he possessed the entire region from the Kentucky River to the Cumberland. He said that he had acquired this claim by a treaty with the Cherokee—the Treaty of Sycamore Shoals, March 1775. The settlers were prompt to point out that the land was never the Cherokees' to give. Neither Virginia nor North Carolina favored establishment of a "new" colony.

These first settlers often brought a slave or two as well as white servants and apprentices. Soon many families had blacks and perhaps a bond servant or hired man. During the war, slaves were also brought to the frontier from the Spanish possessions on the lower Mississippi. Blacks did their share in clearing the frontier. They were often trained in skilled crafts required in the infant settlements. Like their masters, blacks and indentured servants suffered the rigors of life under siege in the forts. They, too, fell victim to Indian attacks as they worked in the fields or accompanied hunting or surveying parties. Some served in the militia when manpower was scarce, and, on occasion, were given noncommissioned rank.

During 1775, the population of the Kentucky stations varied widely, from fifty to three hundred souls, as men located land, returned east to bring out family and friends, or deserted stations when Indian hostility loomed.

On this western frontier, warfare did not really resume until 1777. After Dunmore's defeat of the Shawnee in 1774, the Indians kept an uneasy peace for a time. Though the tribes remained seemingly neutral, renegade Indians, resentful over advancing white settlement, committed isolated depredations and murder. Daniel Boone's party had been attacked in March as they were cutting the Wilderness Road west of the Cumberland Gap. So, too, had another nearby group moving west.

When word of the skirmishes at Lexington and Concord reached the frontier in early summer 1775, patriotism and solidarity were staunchly proclaimed. But few among those who coveted the lands and opportunities of this rich area believed that the British could keep the Indians quiet, even if they tried. Accordingly, hasty efforts were made to organize the region for government, safety, and defense.

George Rogers Clark returned to Virginia in the winter of 1775-1776 to settle his affairs before permanently moving to Kentucky. His activity in the stations the preceding summer had convinced him that people there were not anxious to pay Henderson's prices for land or submit to the Judge's laws for Transylvania. Clark thought they preferred to be attached to Virginia, and, failing that, would support their own, independent regime. Henderson's agents had been attempting to get approval for the new colony from the Continental Congress but that body had refused to act without the approval of Virginia. Clark found opinion among the Virginia gentry divided on the question of the propriety of Henderson's proposal. Therefore it seemed necessary to him that the settlers organize themselves and persuade the new state government to recognize Kentucky as part of Virginia in order to forestall Henderson's plans. Alternately, if Virginia would not accept responsibility for the defense of the new lands, the settlers could make themselves independent of both Virginia and Henderson. To settle the matter, Clark proposed a meeting at Harrodstown for early June, 1776.

§ **Organizing for Defense**

Clark arrived late on the day of the meeting. He found that, rather than debating the pros and cons of independence or connection with Virginia, people there had already voted for the latter. Rejecting Henderson's Transylvania government, which was run on principles far from those for which

rebellious Americans were now ready to fight, they petitioned to become part of Virginia. They elected Clark and John Gabriel Jones to represent them in Virginia's new House of Delegates, affirming their ability to defend the western frontiers of the state and bear their share in the struggle against Britain.

Clark and Jones set out for Williamsburg, the state capital, without delay. Time was running short to prepare adequately for the defense of the frontier. They chose the Wilderness Road, unaware that the Cherokees were about to attack in the southwest, and they traveled alone. Jones's horse gave out. Steady rains so soaked the travelers' feet that they both developed something they called "scald"—their feet burning and swollen so they could hardly walk. Signs of Indian hostility were all around. Seeking help at Martin's Fort, just east of the Cumberland Gap, they found the settlement deserted. In desperation they fortified the strongest cabin. For food they killed one of the hogs left behind by the settlers and laid out their arms and ammunition to defend themselves in case of attack. As they were supping and treating their feet with oil, they were alerted by a jingling horse bell. A group of men had returned from the Clinch River settlement to reclaim some of their goods. Each party mistook the other for Indians. They were much relieved to discover otherwise. With the help of this group, Clark and Jones reached the settled part of Virginia.

There they discovered the Virginia Assembly was not in session so they would have to wait until fall to present their petition. Meanwhile, Clark made efforts to procure ammunition for the frontier. Governor Patrick Henry was at home, ill, but Clark called on him. Henry expressed approval of the Kentucky petition and furnished Clark with an introduction to the gentlemen of the Virginia Council.

Clark met with the Council in late August, asking for five hundred pounds of gunpowder. The Council was sympathetic, but considered it beyond their power to give such supplies until the Assembly had acted to make Kentucky an organized part of Virginia. They proposed to lend the amount, with the cost of transportation falling upon Clark. At this, Clark balked. He had no funds for such expenses. He returned the Council's order for the powder with a sharp letter threatening to withdraw Kentucky's offer to become part of Virginia. He bluntly put it to them that if they thought the "country was not worth protecting it was not worth claiming. . . . " This brought prompt action. The Council ordered the powder from the magazine at Williamsburg delivered to Pittsburgh where Clark might pick it up.

As soon as the Assembly met, Jones joined Clark to present Kentucky's case. Henderson was present to oppose them as was Colonel Arthur Campbell who, as representative from Fincastle County, rejected the notion of a new county being erected in an area which had been considered part of Fincastle. The Assembly would not seat Clark and Jones as representatives but agreed to consider the Kentucky situation. They acted favorably on 7 December, 1776, erecting the area into a new county to be called Kentucky.

Although Clark probably preferred the idea of making Kentucky an independent region, he recognized that annexation by Virginia offered the best chance of offsetting Henderson's domination and favored the speculations in land that Clark, Jones, Isaac Hite, others in the Harrodstown group, and even Governor Henry had been pursuing. Richard Henderson did not give up. He took his case back to the Continental Congress where dispute rumbled over it until Virginia finally gave up its western claims to the federal government late in the war.

Clark and Jones parted at Williamsburg but agreed to meet at Pittsburgh to pick up the gunpowder. It proved to be a dangerous and difficult undertaking to get the powder to Harrodstown. Clark learned at Pittsburgh that the Indians were getting ready to attack in the spring. Even though several tribes had promised neutrality and friendship, the British were now stirring them up. Clark suspected Indians around Fort Pitt were less friendly than they appeared to be and were plotting to waylay his group as soon as they left for Kentucky.

Hastily loading a small vessel, Clark and Jones with only seven men started down the Ohio with the gunpowder so urgently needed by the settlements. Their suspicions were confirmed. Indians were indeed preparing to intercept them. Slipping past the Indians at night, they landed and hid the powder in scattered locations before striking out by land for Harrodstown. At Hinkston's Station on Licking Creek they paused for rest. Colonel John Todd was reported in the area with a force strong enough to return for the powder, but Clark pushed on with two men to Harrodstown for more certain help, leaving Jones and the others. Soon after he had left, Todd's men appeared. With Jones to guide them, they started back for the powder. The Indians who had been pursuing the party surprised them, killing several of the ten men. John Gabriel Jones, who had been chairman of the Harrodstown meeting that declared for Virginia and who had come so far with Clark on this mission to establish the new county, was among those killed on Christmas Day, 1776. Clark's cousin, Joseph Rogers, was captured. The powder remained undiscovered but, as Clark said in his memoirs written many years later, "the loss of a single man at this time was sensibly felt. . . ." Frightened frontiersmen resolutely girded for war, determined to stand their ground.

Clark reached Harrodstown safely. A large party was formed to go after the gunpowder. Successfully locating the cache, they brought the urgently needed kegs to the security of the Kentucky stations.

Indians attacked McClelland's Fort at the end of December. Two settlers, including the founder, John McClelland, perished. By the end of January 1777, that post was abandoned and its people moved into Harrodsburg, as it was now being called. Similarly, the other smaller stations were being deserted as the Kentuckians concentrated in their three strongest posts—Harrodsburg, Boonesborough, and Logan's.

Four

The Struggle for the Indians

While the Kentuckians prepared to defend their frontier and the people of eastern Tennessee fought off the Cherokee, the Congress of the new nation and the government of Virginia combined to take official action to keep the Indians at peace.

In June 1775, Virginia's own Indian commission made preparations to convene the tribes in a meeting at Pittsburgh. During July and August, James Wood, a member of the commission, ranged through the Indian towns of the Shawnee, Wyandot, Ottawa, Delaware, and Seneca, urging them to send representatives to Fort Pitt in September. Through them he also extended the invitation to more distant tribes.

Congress sent its commissioners for the middle district: James Wilson; Lewis Morris, who had replaced Benjamin Franklin; and Dr. Thomas Walker, who had been appointed in place of Patrick Henry. Dr. Walker, a member of both the Virginia and Congressional commissions, served as chairman of the proceedings. An early explorer of Kentucky, he had discovered Cumberland Gap and named it for England's Duke of Cumberland.

The tribes gathered slowly and reluctantly. Some of the chiefs appeared inclined to friendship; others seemed belligerent. Lengthy speeches, in which the commissioners alternately wooed and threatened, and the Indians sometimes responded with sincerity and sometimes without, consumed September and most of October. The upshot of the resulting agreement of 1775 was that the older chiefs would attempt to keep their own and neighboring tribes neutral. But they expressed strong objections to having either the Americans or the British march through or fight in their hunting grounds. The younger leaders, resentful of the haughty frontiersmen and their frequent brutalities against the Indians, were clearly vacillating and would probably join the British.

§ **Uneasy Indian Peace**

At any rate, the negotiations served to keep most of the powerful Shawnee and Delaware quiet for another year and bought that much more time for the Ohio Valley to prepare. The British Lieutenant Governor Henry Hamilton, newly arrived at Detroit in November, sized up the results of the Americans' meeting at Pittsburgh accurately. He wrote to Governor Carleton in Quebec that the Indians "are not likely to continue upon terms with the Virginians. . . . The savages have a high opinion of them as Warriors, but are jealous of their encroachments, and very suspicious of their faith in treaties. . . . The [Virginians] have plundered, burnt, and murdered without mercy. Tis to be supposed from the character of the savages that opportunity only is wanting to retaliate and that there can be but little cordiality between them."

While the commissions met at Pittsburgh, Dr. John Connolly, formerly Dunmore's Indian agent, was hatching an ambitious plot. With the approval of the British commander-in-chief, General Gage, and Lord Dunmore, who had fled Virginia to seek refuge aboard a British man-of-war in the Chesapeake, Connolly proposed to arouse the frontier Loyalists and Indians for an attack on Fort Pitt, after which he would move east against Virginia itself while Dunmore landed with British troops on the Virginia coast, smashing the former colony between the two forces. Had Connolly been successful, the Virginia frontier would have been lost even before America declared independence. If both Connolly and Dunmore had accomplished their goals, Virginia itself would have been lost to the cause. Instead Connolly, too well-known to move west unrecognized, was seized by American patriots and the plot was foiled.

Nevertheless, the frontier on the upper Ohio remained in a precarious position. John Dodge, a trader living with the Wyandots in Sandusky, reported in December 1775 that Lieutenant Governor Hamilton was urging the Indians to make war. Hamilton's position at Detroit was weak: he needed the help of Indians. But he did not, in fact, receive orders to unleash the tribes until a year and a half later, although he began advocating it to his superiors in 1776.

To prepare themselves for what was coming, the settlers around Pittsburgh had organized a government even before Kentucky had been recognized. Virginia men declared themselves as the new county of West Augusta in May 1775, while rival Pennsylvanians meeting at Hannastown a few miles east established the county of Westmoreland. Since the boundary between Pennsylvania and Virginia was not settled until later in the war, these rival jurisdictions hampered the raising of militia. Though the settlers in this area finally achieved a superficial cooperation, their rivalry tended to break out from time to time, interfering with numerous campaigns. When Regulars were subsequently stationed at Fort Pitt, their commanders had continual difficulties managing these factions. The problem was a serious source of weakness for the region around the Forks of the Ohio.

Model of Fort Pitt in the Fort Pitt Museum,
Point State Park, Pittsburgh, Pennsylvania.
Courtesy of the Pennsylvania Historical and Museum
Commission.

Relative peace in the Ohio Valley through most of 1776 freed the militia of the inner Virginia and North Carolina frontiers to deal with the Cherokee uprisings farther south. Nevertheless, occasional outrages occurred, committed by both whites and Indians. Though widely scattered these events kept tension high throughout the spring, summer, and fall.

In the latter part of June the twin sons of Andrew McConnell—Adam and William—were captured and a servant boy with them was killed near Leestown. Friendly Shawnee intervened, exchanging a rifle for the two boys after they spent sixty days as prisoners.

Jemima Boone, fourteen, and her two friends, Betsey and Fanny Callaway, sixteen and fourteen, were seized from a canoe near Boonesborough and carried off early in July. The girls, thoroughly scared, risked the Indians' wrath by surreptitiously leaving a trail of heelprints and bits of clothing. Hanging Maw, the leader, had met Jemima's famous father and was inclined to be tolerant. When their captors caught a small horse for the girls to ride on, they delayed the march by regularly falling off, to the mingled amusement and anger of the Indians. Jemima's father, the doughty Daniel Boone, organized a rescue party which included the young man already engaged to Betsey Callaway. This group caught up with the kidnapers beyond the Licking River three days later and rescued the girls, killing two of the Indians.

Many attacks were the work of a small group of Mingos (western Senecas) living on the Scioto River along with renegades from the Shawnee and Wyandot tribes, led by one Captain Pluggy. Enemies of the Virginians since Dunmore's War, they could not be restrained by the more responsible chiefs who had negotiated with the American agents.

From May onward, the officials at Pittsburgh followed a dual policy. George Morgan, the agent, continued his efforts to bring the Indians in for talks that might keep them neutral. He arranged another treaty conference for October 1776. But, meanwhile, efforts to strengthen the frontier went on. Captain Matthew Arbuckle was sent with Virginia militiamen to garrison Fort Randolph at the mouth of the Kanawha River, guarding the approaches to the inner settlements up the river around the "levels" of Greenbrier in the western mountains. George Gibson and William Linn were sent down the Ohio and Mississippi in order to bring back gunpowder available from the Spanish at New Orleans.

On a broader scale, General Charles Lee, serving as senior officer under Washington in the eastern army, proposed an attack on the British in Detroit. Although Washington approved the idea, Congress dropped the plan when it appeared obvious that such a major campaign would require men, supplies, and preparations beyond the country's capacity. Washington was preparing to defend New York against the main British army. The West could expect no help from his thin and disorganized forces.

The results of the Indian conference in the fall of 1776 gave Morgan some reason for optimism. He reported renewed promises of peace from Seneca, Delaware, and Shawnee. Even Wasson, the Chippewa chief from the far-away Saginaw Valley, had attended.

But Morgan's hopes were not shared by other leaders on the Ohio. In June and July, an Indian trader who worked for Morgan had traveled among the Delaware and Wyandot. This trader, William Wilson, had been openly threatened by Lieutenant Governor Hamilton on a visit to Detroit; White Eyes, a friendly Delaware chief who accompanied Wilson, had been ordered out of the area. A sympathetic Englishman in Detroit, William Tucker, who served as interpreter for the Chippewa and Ottawa, admitted to Wilson that the Indians were planning to attack. Though not openly urging warfare, Hamilton was providing Indians with guns, ammunition, knives, and supplies.

The Indian commissioners at Pittsburgh heard rumors of a threatened attack by fifteen hundred Chippewa and Ottawa along with the possibility that the Potawatomi farther west would also descend on the American frontier. They confessed suspicion of the Wyandot and Seneca tribes as well as the already hostile Mingo. Pluggy's band was obviously on the warpath again despite promises of the Shawnee to pacify them. Pluggy's Mingos and other assorted followers were identified as the group that had attacked Jones and his men while they were attempting to recover the powder at the end of the previous year, the same band that attacked McClelland's Station soon after that.

The county lieutenant of West Augusta reported two women killed and a boy captured on Fish Creek in early October. Another party of whites coming up the Ohio from Kentucky was attacked at the mouth of the Hockhocking River at about the same time. Despite Morgan's optimism,

word of reinforcement of British positions at Detroit, Sandusky, and Niagara was an ominous sign. Many believed that the western Indians would probably attack in the spring. Already some were raiding in hopes that suspicion would fall on the still friendly Delaware and Shawnee, provoking the Americans to break their treaty.

§ British Outposts

However insecure the Americans were, the British were no safer. Though many British leaders hesitated to start a savage Indian war, they were too few to hold their western posts without Indian allies.

Five hundred British soldiers were stretched thin to cover three outposts—Niagara, Detroit, and Michilimackinac. When the Redcoats abandoned Fort Pitt in 1772, they had also withdrawn from Fort Chartres on the Mississippi. The small garrison from Chartres under Captain Hugh Lord had fortified the old Jesuit house in Kaskaskia, but even this outpost was left to its native French inhabitants in May 1776, when Lord and his men were needed to reinforce Detroit.

Before Lord's troops arrived, Detroit had about one hundred twenty Regulars commanded by Captain Richard B. Lernoult. It was supplied largely from Canada. Guns of several small vessels in the Detroit River somewhat increased its defensive strength. Although Hamilton and Lernoult did not expect any immediate attack, they had worked to strengthen the fortifications while Jehu Hay, British Indian agent for the area, labored to win the allegiance of the tribes—just as his counterpart, George Morgan, was doing for the Americans at Pittsburgh. Even Governor Hamilton took an active part in treating with the warriors and seeing to their equipment.

About three hundred fifty able-bodied French inhabitants were incorporated into Detroit's militia but they were neither trained nor drilled. They exhibited even less enthusiasm for fighting than did the Redcoats stationed there. Many of the French had never warmed to their British conquerors; they certainly lacked interest in the British cause.

America's enemies on the frontier were further weakened by the fact that the governor of Canada, Sir Guy Carleton at Quebec, did not get along with his superior in England, Lord George Germain. He resented Germain's dealing directly with his subordinate, Lieutenant Governor Hamilton. In addition, Carleton was too far from Detroit to control Hamilton's actions effectively. Another source of weakness was the fact that Hamilton did not get along well with Edward Abbott, who was awaiting appointment as lieutenant governor of a proposed new British post, Vincennes.

Elsewhere in the region, Major Arent S. dePeyster had only a small body of Redcoats at Michilimackinac. A Frenchman, Philippe Francois de Rastel, Chevalier de Rocheblave, commanded the little fort at Kaskaskia in the Illinois country after Captain Lord departed but had only an inactive French militia he might call upon. Similarly, when Abbott became lieutenant governor at Vincennes, on the Wabash, he was provided with no regular troops. At the important British trading post of Ouiatenon on the upper Wabash another Frenchman, Jean Baptiste Celeron, served as a somewhat untrustworthy British agent as did Charles Beaubien at Miamistown at the head of the Maumee. Louis Chevalier represented the British with the Potawatomi at Fort St. Joseph on the St. Joseph River near Lake Michigan.

Governor Carleton and his successor, General Frederick Haldimand, wanted to limit the use of Indians. Carleton had opposed General Gage's orders to set the warriors against the frontier. As late as 1778 Abbott, after resigning the post at Vincennes, continued to oppose using Indians. He noted that such use probably forced many who might have remained loyal to join the rebels, and pointed out, "It is not people in arms that Indians will ever daringly attack; but the poor inoffensive families who fly to the deserts to be out of trouble and are inhumanely butchered sparing neither women or children."

But faced with the major responsibility, Hamilton urged use of the Indian warriors. Lord George Germain in England, who had to go the German states to hire soldiers to fight for the British in America, saw no reason to object to utilizing Indians although he urged that British leaders accompany them to keep them under control.

Given Britain's numerical inferiority in the West, the thousands of Indians were a resource the British could not do without. Over twelve hundred Delaware, Shawnee, and Mingo occupied Ohio. In lower Michigan and along Lake Erie, three hundred Wyandot, Huron, and six hundred Ottawa were available. North of them were thousands of Chippewa, and several hundred Potawatomi stretched across and towards the lower end of Lake Michigan. North and east of Fort Pitt were Senecas, while on the Maumee and upper Wabash were several hundred Miami. On the Wabash and over towards the Mississippi were more Indians, the Wea, Piankeshaw, Kickapoo, and others. Beyond the Lakes were the Fox, Sauk, Mascouten; no one knew just how many.

Unstable, vacillating, and unreliable, the Indians were not great assets as combatants. Whether they would fight, against whom, and for how long was always a question. They were divided by rivalries among themselves, often unwilling to leave their families for long campaigns, easily frightened when faced by any show of strength. Even their numbers were deceiving. They would rarely fight in any but small groups for limited periods. For the British they did not, in the end, prove to be a decisive military factor. But fighting against the British, they would have made that power's position in the West untenable.

The war in the West was destined to be a defensive war for the most part. Lacking supplies, adequate roads for transportation, without the means to maintain lines of strong forts, both sides would have to rely on guerrilla warfare, sporadic and destructive raids and counterraids against isolated settlements, small garrisons, and Indian towns. Major sustained offensives against primary targets like Detroit or Pittsburgh were never possible with the manpower and equipment available.

The heroes of this frontier war would be the leaders of small forces, maneuvering rapidly on the rivers and in the prairies, or stoutly defending their ill-provisioned forts and cabins. Heroic, too, would be the men in the ranks who followed their leaders on seemingly hopeless missions, enduring privation and danger, often miserable and complaining but carrying on. And the women and children who stuck it out in the frontier stations were no less courageous than the men who fought. Disease, starvation, and sudden death accompanied everyone in this small but total warfare in the West. Ordinary men and women fought for their futures and lives. They were their country's agents of empire.

Indian Tribes on the Western Frontier.

Five

War Comes to the Frontier

The "Year of the Three Sevens" became the "Bloody Year" on the western border. Indian warfare, savage and brutal, broke in full fury. It was more formidable and relentless than before because it was British-led and British-supplied.

At Detroit, Hamilton had received the answer to his request. In Britain, Lord George Germain, secretary of state for the colonies, ordered the Indians unleashed. Now the tribes which had been chafing at the restraints put on them would be urged to attack the "Big Knives," as the Indians called American frontiersmen.

On 17 June, 1777, Hamilton convened the Ottawa, Huron, Chippewa, Potawatomi, Miami, Shawnee, and Delaware. Painted and dressed like an Indian himself, Hamilton personally sang the war song, exhorted the Indians to attack, and set out a feast for them. Huge amounts of food, ammunition, guns, scalping knives, war paint, and other supplies were provided. Though Hamilton warned the Indians against attacking old men, women, and children, he boasted of having a thousand Indians ready to fight. British or French-Canadian leaders who would accompany them were clearly too few to restrain them.

Already Lieutenant Governor Edward Abbott had set out for Vincennes to enlist the warriors of the Wabash, although he had little stomach for the task. When he left Detroit, Abbott was escorted by a few Piankeshaw chiefs who came from Vincennes to meet him. A small body of French militia and several Ottawa and Chippewa braves went along. At Miamistown (the present Fort Wayne, Indiana) twenty-four residents of his new post arrived to greet him, as well as more Indians of the Wea, Piankeshaw, Mascouten, and Kickapoo tribes and a few Shawnee and Delaware. To about five hundred Indians, Abbott passed out the expected presents with a lavish hand. Crossing over to the Wabash from the Maumee he discovered that without a large body of troops to awe the Indians he must continue to distribute gifts as he moved down the river.

The new British commander arrived at Vincennes (or St. Vincent's, as it was often called) on 19 May. Eighty or ninety French families lived there, but the town had no stockade or garrison. Abbott was expected to keep the Indians in the British interest, enlist them to fight, and attempt to prevent supplies from reaching the Americans from New Orleans. Yet he was given no regular troops. Governor Carleton was soon complaining about the high cost of his presents to the Indians.

Abbott promptly organized the men of the town into three companies of militia, about one hundred and fifty in all, and constructed a shaky palisade to serve as a fort around the cabin in which he lived—as much for his own protection against the Indians as it was for defense against the enemy. The Miami had turned down Hamilton's offer of the hatchet, nor did the Indians of the Wabash seem very eager to fight the Long Knives. They were under the influence of the French inhabitants, who had little interest in the war. Discouraged by his inability to be effective, harassed about the expense of his post, and fearful for his own safety, Abbott remained at Vincennes less than a year. He set out for Detroit in February 1778, leaving his little "Fort Sackville" to its French militia.

He had named the fort for the British secretary of state, Lord George Germain, formerly known as Lord Sackville.

Notwithstanding Abbott's failure to effect Britain's objectives, Hamilton was doing quite enough. By September 1777, he recorded having sent out over a thousand warriors. A scant twenty prisoners had been brought in out of almost eighty who he knew had been captured. Any argument over whether Hamilton was a "hair buyer" or not is futile. To the Virginians, the mere fact that he gave the Indians lavish supplies, aroused them with blood-curdling speeches, provided them with guns and knives along with too few white leaders to control them, with but mild cautions about restraint, made him the "Hair-Buyer General." A spy from Pittsburgh heard from Hamilton's Indian translator that the governor did not try very hard to redeem captives but paid high prices for scalps.

It was all part of the British master plan for 1777. General Burgoyne was marching along Lake Champlain towards New England and New York. General Howe in New York was supposed to move northward to meet him. Indians, Canadians, and Loyalists struck at the Mohawk Valley border between Niagara and Albany, while Hamilton launched the Indians against the settlements on the Allegheny, Monongahela, upper Ohio, and in Kentucky.

§ **Frontier Defense**

With everything pointing to all-out Indian war, the militia leaders around Pittsburgh prepared to fight. The Virginia government had reorganized West Augusta County into three new counties: Monongahela, Ohio, and Yough-iogheny. Their county lieutenants called up their militia. The major settlements south of Pittsburgh along the Ohio River were provided with small garrisons at Beech Bottom, Wheeling, and Grave Creek.

In March the Virginia government ordered three hundred militia from this area to attack the Mingo and Shawnee renegades at Pluggy's Town. George Morgan, hoping to keep his treaty with the Indians in force, feared such an invasion across the Ohio would provoke widespread alarm among heretofore friendly tribes. Congress, upon his representation, ordered the expedition canceled. But recognizing the dangers to the frontier, Congress authorized a force of Regulars to augment the militia of Virginia and Pennsylvania at Fort Pitt, and ordered Washington to select a commander. General Edward Hand, M.D., arrived on 1 June to take command.

In May Captain William Linn had arrived with a large shipment of gunpowder from New Orleans where he and George Gibson had gone a year earlier. To placate the British, the Spanish had detained Gibson in New Orleans but permitted Linn to start up the Mississippi with nine thousand pounds of powder which they supplied. When Linn's boats reached the mouth of the Ohio, they received necessary support from agents of Thomas Bentley, an American sympathizer who operated a trading venture at Kaskaskia. This aid infuriated Rocheblave, the commander for the British at Kaskaskia, who later arranged for Bentley's arrest and detention in Canada. But the powder had come safely to the

magazines on the upper Ohio. Gibson was also on his way by ship to the east coast with additional supplies for General Washington.

With an adequate supply of ammunition and a new commander, the northern Ohio frontier was ready for defense, although many persons, including General Hand and Governor Patrick Henry, favored taking the war to the Indians instead of awaiting their attack.

The upper Ohio region was spared any major assault until late in the summer of 1777. Detroit's war parties descended on the Kentucky settlements early in March, not turning to the Ohio River posts until August. By this time, isolated murders and ominous threats from occasional "friendly" Indian visitors had aroused widespread alarm. People were "forting up" and many fearful families prepared to return east. Others were swayed by notices left along the trails, at the sites of burned cabins, and beside bodies of scalped victims, urging Americans to declare for Britain and move to Detroit. Finding packages of these propaganda leaflets sent out by Governor Hamilton, many frontier officers hid them away fearing they might prove all too persuasive to the fearful settlers.

The storm broke at Logstown, a small trading post downstream and across from Pittsburgh where a soldier was killed and a boy taken. A handful of men surprised and killed an Indian lurking near Wheeling; more Indians were reported on Sandy River; a white couple was killed near Elk Creek. General Hand began receiving reports of raids and war parties all around the area. Two Negro slaves were

General Edward Hand, M.D. (1744-1802). General Hand commanded at Fort Pitt from June 1, 1777, to July 1778. He was born in Ireland, emigrated to America in 1767, and settled at Lancaster, Pennsylvania.

Courtesy of The Historical Society of Pennsylvania.

wounded near Wheeling. With Governor Henry's approval, Hand sought to raise more troops from the interior Virginia settlements, but Indians threatened as far away as the Clinch River and Loyalists were reported to be planning to seize the principal powder supply at Redstone Fort, up the Monongahela. With but a dozen or so defenders, most places were reluctant to provide soldiers for Hand.

Fort Henry at Wheeling was struck on 1 September—first of several attacks on it during the war. Four or five hundred soldiers had been concentrated there in anticipation of an attack, and the fort was the strongest on the Ohio except for Fort Pitt. But when Indians did not immediately appear, most of the soldiers were withdrawn, leaving fewer than one hundred. Andrew Zane with a few men had gone up the hill back of the fort to bring in some livestock belonging to a Dr. McMechan, who was preparing to move back to the Monongahela. A small party of braves attempted to seize the group. Zane jumped over a bluff and escaped to a blockhouse some miles away. One man was tomahawked, but Loudon, a slave belonging to Dr. McMechan, dashed to the fort with the alarm. Displaying a rashness all too common in the early months of the war, about twenty men rushed out of the fort to attack. They ignored a warning received from General Hand that this war party was a large one.

Indeed, it numbered about two hundred. The little group moving out of the fort was drawn around the hill into a carefully planned ambush. Fifteen were killed and five wounded. The Indians—Mingo, Wyandot, and some Shawnee—then rushed the fort. Fog hung over the settlement and the Indians added to the murk by setting the town ablaze. The defenders complained that the women, struggling to see through the gunports what had happened to their men, got in the way. But the women "ran bullets in frying pans. . . . Mrs. Duke cut bullet patches . . . like one cutting out shirts. And one Scotchman prayed all day. . . . The women brought up water in tubs and scrubbed [drenched] the roofs," to put out the fires. Nineteen-year-old William Shepherd, son of the fort's commander, struggling to get back to the stockade, caught his foot in a grapevine, was slain and scalped. Colonel Shepherd's son-in-law, Francis Duke, coming to help from the Beech Bottom Fort, was shot down trying to make the gate. When night fell, the Indians abandoned their attack, leaving cabins and fields burned, property looted, and the neighborhood littered with carcasses of cattle, hogs, sheep, and horses.

At Pittsburgh, Hand now determined to attack. With authority from the Virginia and Pennsylvania governments, he called for troops and prepared to take the war to the enemy. Protests reached Governor Henry that such an attack might only make matters worse. The governor agreed with Hand that Indian depredations were already so serious that the existence of the frontier was at stake. The harassed Kentucky stations could not spare men, nor was there much inclination to provide militia from the sparsely defended inner settlements on the Greenbrier and Kanawha between Fort Pitt and Kentucky. Hand also found himself competing

Fort Henry on the Ohio River at Wheeling was built in 1774. It was first called Fort Fincastle and was attacked by the British and by Indians in 1777 and 1782. The latter attack was the last battle between British soldiers and American militia, and took place September 11.

Courtesy of the State Historical Society of Wisconsin.

with General Washington, who was drafting men to oppose Howe's march on Philadelphia. Hand's offensive did not appear very promising.

By mid-September, Hand was forced to withdraw the garrison from his outpost at Kittanning, north of Pittsburgh, in favor of manning a smaller post between the Allegheny and Kiskeminetas rivers. He named this post Fort Hand. At Wheeling, Fort Henry had only twenty men fit for duty. News of Burgoyne's defeat at Saratoga aroused hope that it might slow Indian attacks, but few friendly Indians now came to parley with the agent, George Morgan. The wrath of whites at Fort Pitt against the braves was so great that Morgan had to put up the Indians in his own house to protect them from settlers. White Eyes, the friendly Delaware chief, reported that the Wyandots were openly threatening those Indians who maintained relations with Pittsburgh.

Late in the month Captains William Foreman, William Linn, and Joseph Ogle took a party to reconnoiter the site of an abandoned fort at Grave Creek. On their march back, a few miles south of Wheeling, they were caught in ambush. Foreman and twenty men were killed. One who escaped said the tomahawks sounded "as if the Indians were cutting up beef."

Savagery was not confined to one side. Much Tory activity was evident in the valleys east of Pittsburgh on the Monongahela and Youghiogheny. Aroused patriots seized one of the Loyalist leaders, Hickson or Higginson, and carried him bound across the Cheat River. Colonel Zackwell Morgan, the county lieutenant, dumped him in the river, where he drowned. Morgan's men threatened to refuse to fight if their leader was convicted of this outrage, so Morgan went free. Tense frontiersmen suspected treachery even in high places. At one time both George Morgan and General Hand were thought to have British leanings.

In October the friendly Shawnee chief, the Cornstalk, came to Fort Randolph accompanied by two other chiefs, Redhawk and Old Yie. Sadly but fatalistically, Cornstalk announced that his tribe was yielding to British pressure. The chiefs would have to go along with them. Cornstalk forecast that he would be killed, offering to allow the commander, Captain Arbuckle, to kill him then and there. Arbuckle had no wish to hurt the chief who had been faithful so long in holding his tribe to pledges of amity. He could but detain him and the others as hostages. Cornstalk's son soon arrived, looking for his father, and he too remained.

§ **Assaults on the Indians**

One morning early in November, two men of a company from Botetourt County serving at Point Pleasant crossed the Kanawha to hunt. Lurking Indians shot and scalped one of them. The other ran wildly to the bank of the river across from the fort, calling to soldiers who had heard the shot. The men brought the bloody body back. Led by their captain, Hall, they stormed past the protesting Arbuckle, entered the cabin where Cornstalk was staying, and shot the Indian as he soberly rose to meet them. His son, sitting nearby, was riddled with bullets. Redhawk, trying to escape up the chimney, was pulled down and killed and Old

Yie was savagely hacked to pieces. From that time on, the once friendly Shawnee became the inveterate enemies of the Americans.

Both General Hand and Governor Henry were shocked by the outrage. Henry suggested that the attack on Cornstalk was a Tory plot to loose the Shawnee against the frontier to prevent westerners from coming east to reinforce Washington. Nonetheless, he ordered the guilty punished. It was as easily argued that the Indians who killed the soldier did it to arouse the Virginians to kill Cornstalk and thus swing the Shawnee away from their lukewarm friendship with the Americans. At any rate, although it was well known that Captain Hall and his men had done the deed in defiance of Captain Arbuckle's orders, witnesses refused to testify. Despite Henry's urging, the culprits were never convicted.

Meeting with the officers of Virginia and Pennsylvania during October and November, General Hand came to the conclusion that he could not gather enough men to march against the Ohio Indians. Warriors still roamed the woods and rivers in the vicinity, forcing militia leaders to keep their men at home for defense. The weather had turned too cold for the troops, who lacked adequate clothing, to venture out. Hand canceled his planned offensive. He also asked to be recalled, in view of his inability to enlist and equip enough men for a more active role, or to reconcile quarreling factions of Virginia and Pennsylvania.

Before Congress acted on his request, Hand was called upon to initiate two more efforts. The first was to help James Willing and a company of men start on a raid down the Ohio to the British posts on the lower Mississippi. Willing held a captain's commission in the Continental Navy. His forces manning the armed boat *Rattletrap* were also to bring back more powder and provisions from the Spanish at New Orleans. On 10 January, 1778, Willing was on his way.

The second move was to carry out a request from Governor Henry to make some diversion in connection with George Rogers Clark's campaign. In February 1778, Hand crossed the Ohio and marched north towards the Cuyahoga with a large force made up, for the most part, of Pennsylvania militia. Finding only some small, almost deserted Indian towns (near the present New Castle, Pennsylvania), Hand achieved nothing. His men attacked a small group of women, children and only one man at one town but most of them escaped. Part of Hand's force struck at another defenseless village and killed three women and a boy. Among the wounded was the mother of the friendly Delaware, Captain Pipe. Pipe's brother was killed. Again, the Americans had undone what little the Indian councils at Pittsburgh had achieved. Hand admitted that his men had been out of control. This dismal performance by a disproportionately large force became mockingly known as the "Squaw Campaign."

General Hand's cup of bitterness ran over when Alexander McKee and Simon Girty fled Pittsburgh, where they had long been suspected of Loyalist sympathies, and joined the British. Both became highly effective leaders of the Indians, feared and hated among the Americans as few others. Girty joined his brothers, George and James, all of whom had lived with the Indians after being captured in their youth. Their name became a watchword for treason and savagery in the West. Another brother, Thomas, remained faithful to the United States.

Chagrined by the murder of the Shawnee chiefs at Fort Randolph, humiliated at the result of the Squaw Campaign, and now embarrassed by the escape of McKee and Girty, General Hand must have been relieved when Congress responded to his wish for recall and appointed a new commander for Fort Pitt in May 1778. Hand was an able officer and had tried sincerely to moderate the partisanship around Pittsburgh and to raise a force for a major attack on Detroit. Disappointed by frequent desertions, handicapped by the constant shortages of men and materiel, and hurt by the suspicions and quarrels of his subordinates, he had concluded that "the Devil has possessed both the country and the garrison."

§ Clark Leads Kentucky Defense

In the spring of 1777 the Kentucky settlements had braced for war. George Rogers Clark, only twenty-four, was the senior officer present, carrying the rank of major in the Virginia militia. Already recognized as a leader by his fellow frontiersmen, Clark directed the concentration of settlers in the three strongest stations, Harrodsburg, Boonesborough, and Logan's. By 5 March, the militia had been organized for the defense of these outposts under their various officers.

Further concentration was out of the question. It might have been easier to combine in defense of just one fort, but the yield of crops and availability of game in any one region limited the numbers who could be accommodated at each station and required at least the three strongest ones to be maintained. As it was, people suffered from crowding and grew restless as Indian attacks penned them up during the long summer.

Preparations came none too soon. On 6 March, the day after the militia were formed, Chief Blackfish with two hundred Shawnee warriors began the harassment of the settlements. Simon Kenton, scouting for Clark, sent word to Harrodsburg of impending attack, but arrived at Boonesborough to find the Indians already lurking about. Both at Harrodsburg and Boonesborough, defenders at first made the all-too-frequent mistake of rushing out after small groups of Indians who attacked men working outside the stockades, only to find themselves fighting with a much larger group hidden nearby.

On 24 April Daniel Boone and a dozen men rushed out of their fort to repel Indians and were overwhelmed and nearly cut off. Boone led a charge back to the gate but broke his ankle and had to be carried inside by the youthful Simon Kenton. The indomitable Kenton twice struck down Indians who were about to kill Boone. At Harrodsburg, defenders sallied forth after Indians seized a boy, but they were fortunate that no large force was lurking in the neighborhood.

All summer Chief Blackfish struck alternately at Harrodsburg, Boonesborough, and Logan's, rarely remaining for more than a day or two at a time, with his braves divided into various groups. Without cannon, he could not penetrate the defenses of the forts, but he destroyed the settlers' crops and killed or scattered their livestock. The stations' scouts and hunters met with death or capture. People venturing out to bring in corn or cattle often fell victim to the tomahawk or scalping knife. Food became scarce and the number of able-bodied fighting men dwindled. Clark recalled that at Harrodsburg, "the defense of our forts, the procuring of provisions, and, when possible, surprising the Indians . . . burying the dead and dressing the wounded, seemed to be all our business."

Like Hand, on the upper Ohio, Clark became convinced that the best defense of the frontier would be to carry the war into the enemy's country. Towards the end of April, he had sent off Benjamin Linn and Samuel Moore, in the guise of hunters, to assess the strength of Kaskaskia in the Illinois country and Vincennes on the Wabash. Clark professed to believe that the French commander, Rocheblave, was supplying some of the warriors who were roaming around the Kentucky stations. Assuming that the superior command at Pittsburgh would logically be the one to undertake a major attack on the British at Detroit, Clark may have viewed the Illinois country as an area which the forces he might raise could attack. On 22 June the two men returned with the information Clark wanted.

As the summer wore on, Clark busied himself with militia affairs and came to decisions that would have great consequences for the West. Already excited by the beauty and opportunity the area offered, he also formulated arguments for defense and expansion of American interests there as a vital part of the struggle for a new nation. He saw it as

strategically important for the success of American arms in the East. But all was not hard fighting or sober contemplation. Soon after Linn returned from the Illinois towns, Clark recorded the marriage of the young lieutenant amidst "great merriment."

In August Colonel John Bowman arrived with a hundred men to relieve the hard-pressed stations. The next month Major William Bailey Smith came from the North Carolina frontier with nearly fifty mounted men and a promise of more. Confronted with such numbers, most of the Indians turned their attention to outposts on the upper Ohio.

Roving bands of warriors still harassed the settlements. With winter coming, there were many people who chose to stick it out or were unable to flee back to the safety of settled country. The dirt, disease, and hunger of crowded stations threatened their existence as much as did the Indians. In the long run, defense would not avail. Clark knew this, so on 1 October he left Harrodsburg, joined a large party of men, women, and children from Logan's Station who were giving up the struggle, and started back for Virginia through the Cumberland Gap and across the Appalachians.

In his memoir written many years later, Clark recalled that when he left, "I plainly saw that every eye was turned towards me as if expecting some stroke in their favor." Some thought he was giving up and would join the eastern army. Clark did have in mind a stroke that would, he believed, secure the West. He had decided it was time to put aside any private interests and pledge himself to fight for the public cause. He promised his fellow Kentuckians that he would return.

Two views of the modern reconstruction of Fort Harrodsburg, Harrodsburg, Kentucky. From this fort, George Rogers Clark directed the defense of Kentucky during the summer of 1777.

Six

Clark Plans a Campaign

Clark had written to Governor Patrick Henry sometime during the summer of 1777, after his spies had returned from scouting the Illinois country. With assurance he proposed an expedition to capture Kaskaskia. The British had left the town to Rocheblave, who commanded only a local French militia nominally loyal to the British but largely untrained. Kaskaskia had a "small but elegant stone fort"—the old Jesuit house which Captain Hugh Lord had stockaded with blockhouses at each corner—but since the departure of Lord and the British garrison, it was without soldiers or guards.

Kaskaskia's small cannon, stores, and trade potential made it a tempting target. Even if the French put up a fight, Clark wrote Henry, they could not risk staying in their fort for fear the Americans would burn their village and their provisions. In the unlikely event that they mustered sufficient numbers and energy to defeat him, Clark and his men could take refuge with the friendly Spanish across the Mississippi. The expedition would cost very little. Clark assured the governor that he could raise enough men and, given secrecy, drop down the Ohio to the Wabash or beyond, march swiftly to Kaskaskia, and overwhelm the French in a night attack.

The advantages were many. To delay a strike against the area, whose Indians were being aroused by Rocheblave, would ultimately cost ten times as much, according to Clark. Control of the Illinois country would give the Americans a secure hold on the supply route up the Mississippi and Ohio rivers from New Orleans. "It would fling the command of the two great rivers into our hands. . . ." Clark was hopeful of winning over the French, once he had the chance to explain the American cause to them. Through their influence he might win the tribes of the Mississippi and Wabash from the British, preventing these Indians from attacking Kentucky. He also argued that possession of the Illinois villages would deprive Detroit of supplies from that quarter.

This was the plan that had taken shape in Clark's mind during the weeks that Harrodsburg lay under almost daily attack. "The whole of my time," Clark later recalled, when not busy with defense he had been "reflecting on things in general, particularly Kentucky and how it accorded with the interest of the United States. . . . " It may be that Clark had knowledge of the Illinois country beyond what Linn and Moore had brought to him. When Lieutenant William Linn came up the Mississippi with powder from New Orleans, an agent of Thomas Bentley in Kaskaskia met Linn at the mouth of the Ohio and may have conveyed the idea of an American attack on Kaskaskia. Bentley traded with both the British and the Americans, suffering the displeasure of Rocheblave for his divided loyalties. It may be significant that Clark picked Benjamin Linn, William's brother, to spy for him. Benjamin had probably been to Kaskaskia before.

Further, though Bentley was on a trading venture in the northern Great Lakes when Clark's spies came to Kaskaskia, the trader had advised his associate, Daniel Murray, to expect their arrival. Murray himself was in touch with the Americans through his brother, a patriot sympathizer in New Orleans. Though Bentley was detained in Canada on suspicion of American leanings, Murray and other traders at Kaskaskia gave unstinting support when Clark seized that post. Rocheblave later called Bentley the traitor who sold out the town to the Americans. Certainly both William Linn and Captain George Gibson had opportunity to convey information from these sources to Clark after they returned from New Orleans. The supplies they brought from the Spanish helped to equip Clark's expedition a year later. In addition, John Rogers, a cousin of Clark who served with him on the Illinois campaign, was a close friend of Thomas Bentley.

At any rate, Clark's decision that Kentucky would best be defended by an attack must have agreed well with Governor Henry's thinking. The governor had been urging General Hand to undertake an offensive. As Clark left Logan's Fort in the fall of 1777 to return to Virginia he could be assured of a sympathetic hearing for his proposal.

Clark had just passed his twenty-fifth birthday. Descended from seventeenth-century English planters in Virginia, he was born on a farm along the Rivanna River just east of Charlottesville, the second of ten children. When George Rogers Clark was five, his family moved back to Caroline County and at eleven he was sent to a small private school where James Madison was one of the other students. He found little joy in school and was sent home after a few months. His real training came from his grandfather, John Rogers, who taught him surveying, and from the school of experience on the frontier where he spent most of his time from the age of nineteen.

From all accounts, Clark was tall, well-built, probably with sandy or reddish hair. No early portrait of him exists but the comments about him suggest that he possessed a winning personality and made an impressive appearance. His self-confidence was reflected in the confidence others placed in him.

§ **Expedition to Kaskaskia**

Beyond the Cumberland Gap, Clark left the company

he was traveling with and hurried on alone to his parents' house north of Richmond in Caroline County, a modest plantation with a small number of slaves. Nearly a month on his journey, he had covered over six hundred miles. Parties usually moved at a rate of from fifteen to twenty miles a day, sometimes delaying to hunt. Clark's group had detected signs of Indians near Cumberland Gap but was large enough to discourage attack.

After spending two days with his family, Clark hurried on to Williamsburg, where he devoted most of the remaining month to arranging for the payments due the Kentucky militia. He returned for two weeks with his parents and then went back to the capital to lay his plans before the governor and Council. Henry was enthusiastic, although troubled by the dangers a body of men would face so far from its base. Complete secrecy seemed the only way to ensure the safety of the enterprise; that meant not revealing the objective to the lower house of the legislature, where it would become public knowledge. The House voted approval for a bill merely to permit Clark to raise troops for a vaguely worded project to defend Kentucky. Details were known only to the governor, the Council, and a few influential gentlemen, friends of Clark, who were let in on the plans.

The Council authorized the expedition against Kaskaskia, enjoining "as little delay and as much secrecy as possible." Accordingly Henry issued secret instructions to Clark on 2 January, 1778, to raise three hundred fifty men in seven companies to attack Kaskaskia. Full citizenship and the protection of the United States were to be offered to the French inhabitants. Clark would obtain the necessary boats and stores of war from General Hand at Pittsburgh. The governor reemphasized the need for secrecy, stressing it again in his request to Hand to provide Clark with all possible help.

Three men of standing in Virginia had encouraged Clark and Henry to proceed in this matter. One was George Mason, a Clark family friend of long standing. Mason was an eminent lawyer, an older man from whom the young George Rogers Clark had learned much, and in whom he confided. Another was Thomas Jefferson, a former neighbor of the Clarks but enough older than George Rogers Clark so that the two men probably had not known each other in their youth. The third was George Wythe, who had directed Jefferson's study of law and whom Jefferson called "the honor of his own, and the model of future times." These men acted on the larger stage of national politics, but were also, at this time, off and on members of the Virginia House. They were probably the only members of that body who had been taken into the plan. They assured Clark that if the expedition were successful they could get the Assembly to grant three hundred acres of land to each volunteer, in addition to regular pay.

Clark's stated motives for the expedition may be questioned. The arguments he had outlined to Governor Henry and repeated to the Council did not seem to reflect the realities of military strategy. If Detroit was the major British base, why was Clark planning to attack in almost the opposite direction? Were not the Illinois villages merely phantom targets? The British had not considered them worth garrisoning. Contrary to Clark's assertion, Rocheblave had

Patrick Henry (1736-1799), Governor of Virginia, June 1776 to June 1779. Portrait by Thomas Sully.
Colonial Williamsburg Photograph.

succeeded in enlisting only a few Indians in the British cause. Nor was Detroit provisioned and supplied from these outposts, but rather from its own immediate vicinity and from Canada. The British could not control traffic on the Mississippi and Ohio from Kaskaskia, which Rocheblave admitted when Linn found safe passage and even help from Kaskaskia traders in his journey up these rivers.

What safety for the frontier did Clark expect from a successful attack on these defenseless French villages? With the senior command at Fort Pitt designated to carry the war to Detroit, a mission which General Hand had so far failed to accomplish, did Clark hope to outflank his superiors and win the glory for himself by approaching Detroit from new bases farther west? Did he envisage the need for artillery to knock down defenses at Detroit? Artillery could be carried by water via the Wabash and Maumee rivers, whereas it would be extremely difficult to transport overland from Fort Pitt.

Clark later confessed to Mason that after taking Kaskaskia he expected to win over the French, gain the support of the Indians, and thereby achieve clear passage to move on Detroit. According to his information, the British there were far weaker than the Virginia government believed. He dared not broach this extension of his plan even to Governor Henry, who adhered to the popular view that thousands of men would be needed for such a major objective. The governor would have thought him mad.

That Clark may have hinted at broader objectives is indicated, for in Henry's letter in mid-January the governor issued supplementary orders to "proceed as you find the interest of your country directs . . . to the enemy's settlements above or across, as you may find it proper." Clark considered this approval enough, "to carry my arms to any quarter I pleased." He thought to "undeceive the public respecting their formidable enemies on our frontiers. . . . " Even earlier, in private conversations, Henry had assured Clark that he need not adhere strictly to his written instructions.

Apart from the military advantages Clark anticipated, more personal reasons influenced his move. Despite his youth, Clark was already recognized as a leader. He had been entrusted with the management of public affairs for some time past. His commanding presence, talent for leadership, and thoughtful, capable management had led his fellow settlers to follow him. Loving the country and anticipating its opportunities for profit in land and trade, he could nourish ambition for official preferment, yet he knew that if military glory did not present itself, he could return to his pursuit of personal profit. Like other frontier leaders, he had discovered that wartime service often meant the sacrifice of private affairs.

His game, as he admitted to Mason, was to refuse offers of help from his friends in obtaining promotion. Having proposed an expedition only he, among all the frontier leaders, had visualized or could carry out, he had appeared before the Council as reluctant to solicit its command. He was probably playing "hard to get," lest the government should fail to offer the support the campaign required. Once convinced he had full backing, he had graciously accepted command and a promotion to lieutenant colonel, "Clothed with all the authority I wished for."

It may be that Clark's choice of target was based on his own hopes to establish land claims in the rich region beyond the Ohio as well as to confirm Virginia's right to the region. The state might consider recognition of its expansion in the direction of the Mississippi more likely than a claim for the area farther north around Detroit.

Evidence that profit in land was a motive for both Clark and Governor Henry lies in a land partnership formed by the two men just the day after Clark received his orders. It may also be significant that after his successful march Clark sent ten thousand pounds to his father, remarking, "if Dicky [his younger brother] and myself should both be lost in this country it will be worth seven years trouble of my brothers to seek after my fortune which at this time can't be less than twenty thousand pounds sterling," adding, "my success in trade has been equal to that of war." The amount, not in depreciated paper currency values but in sterling, was indeed a substantial fortune.

If Clark was motivated by selfish reasons as well as zeal for the interests of his country, so were many of the most eminent Revolutionary leaders, who never ceased to be concerned about their private fortunes. Washington, Mason, and Franklin, among others, were deeply involved in speculative western land schemes. Much worse, other well-known patriots in Congress and other government offices continually engaged in activities that amounted to outright war profiteering.

In short, though he claimed long afterward that he had resolved even before coming to Williamsburg to "lay aside every private view," and work solely for the public welfare, Clark had hardly neglected his own interests. But he was also, as he noted, willing to die for his country if America's cause required it. Fortunately his personal ambitions coincided with the public interest. Whatever it may have lacked in initial logic, his expedition proved highly advantageous to the new country.

Far from being an ill-conceived and hazardous expedition, the stroke Clark was preparing was at least so improbable and unsuspected as to offer good hope for success. In view of the utter failure up to that time of plans to attack Detroit, some other offensive thrust was called for. The fears mixed with Governor Henry's enthusiasm were largely unfounded. Clark knew some things that provide a key to understanding his imaginative concept and his confidence in success.

He knew the British had been only partially successful in winning over the Indians, despite the suffering they had inflicted on Kentucky which Clark had himself endured. Though the tribes had their own grievances against the Americans, if Clark could demonstrate that the British could not control the area northwest of the Ohio the Indians might waver, might listen to the Long Knives, or at least stay neutral.

Clark also knew that the Spanish west of the Mississippi were inclined to help the Americans. If hard-pressed, his forces could escape across the river without the risk of a long retreat through hostile territory. If successful, Clark could expect support from Virginia's unofficial agent in New Orleans, Oliver Pollock, who would send supplies directly up the river to the Illinois villages.

In addition, France was daily expected to make an alliance with the United States. Would not this bring the French inhabitants to his side? When news of the actual alliance reached Clark before he started away from the Falls of the Ohio, he became confident that he had a good chance for a friendly reception at Kaskaskia. There was a likelihood that the new connection with France would swing over even the large French population at Detroit.

Finally, Clark had a good intelligence service. He knew Kaskaskia's strengths and weaknesses. Later, when he moved against Vincennes, he had a comprehensive report of Hamilton's strength there from the St. Louis trader, Francis Vigo. Others, Frenchmen and Indians as well as his own scouts, kept him informed of British activities throughout his period of leadership. Hard facts may often have been lacking, but the prairie and river "grapevine" carried amazingly accurate rumors with striking speed from Mackinac to New Orleans.

§ Clark Readies Forces

Clark started west from his father's house about the middle of January 1778. As he moved towards Fort Pitt where he had been assured of getting supplies and ammunition, he appointed officers to recruit the men he needed. Captain William Bailey Smith had been sent to the southwestern

settlements on the Holston to raise men. Clark selected former companions in arms who had been with him in Kentucky and on the Ohio to recruit in the old back country of Virginia and around Pittsburgh. They included Leonard Helm, Joseph Bowman, and William Harrod, who were to assemble at Redstone (now Brownsville, Pennsylvania) on the Monongahela.

General Hand cooperated fully with Clark and was probably in on the full nature of his plans, as were Clark's captains. But many, who heard only the public purpose—to protect the Kentucky settlements—resisted the effort to draw men away from the posts on the upper Ohio or from the southwestern settlements on the Holston, Watauga, and Greenbrier. Attacks in these areas were continuing; with the coming of spring they were expected to intensify.

In addition, secret British sympathizers in and around Pittsburgh obstructed Clark's efforts as did the jealous Pennsylvania men to whom Kentucky meant nothing. This partisanship handicapped Clark just as it had Hand. Many leading men, wrote Clark, "had liked to have put an end to the enterprise, not knowing my destination, and through a spirit of obstinacy they combined and did everything in their power to stop the men that had enlisted, and set the whole frontiers in an uproar, even condescended to harbor and protect those that deserted. . . . "

The longer Clark waited the worse the situation became. Assurances from Smith that he would have four companies from the southwestern settlements were encouraging, although Smith modified his pledge in late March, describing problems similar to Clark's in recruiting. Hopeful that Smith's men would give him the full complement he needed, Clark started with the levies he had. On 12 May he left Redstone, moved to Fort Pitt to pick up his stores, and embarked in boats for the trip down the Ohio. Of the three hundred fifty men he had hoped for, he had only three companies, one hundred fifty in all. It was a Virginia project. Few Pennsylvanians had enlisted, and General Hand, with only a small garrison of Regulars, had provided no Continental soldiers.

It may well be, as Clark later stated, that he "plainly saw that [his] principal design was baffled. . . . " But this was his own ambitous plan to take Detroit, ultimately. For the immediate expedition against Kaskaskia he was full of confidence. "I was always too jealous of myself to be far wrong in plans that I had so long studied. . . . "

At Fort Randolph, the little legion found Captain Arbuckle still reeling from an attack by over two hundred Indians the day before. The war party had moved on, supposedly to attack the Greenbrier settlements far up the Kanawha. Arbuckle wanted Clark's men to follow and attempt an attack. The young commander was tempted, but concluded that he could risk no losses nor take further time without putting his own project in jeopardy.

Moving on to the mouth of the Kentucky, Clark decided against making that his base and instead proceeded to the Falls of the Ohio (now Louisiville, Kentucky) to establish a position to link the Kentucky settlements with the Illinois and defend the navigation of the Ohio.

To Clark's utter disappointment, he now learned that only one company, and that understrength, had arrived from Smith on the Holston. With Clark, predictably, "this information made me as desperate as I was before determined." Of course, he knew that Washington had been desperately drafting men for the eastern army. Nor could he blame Kentuckians for their unwillingness to strip their already undermanned and threatened forts for a project that had not even been disclosed to them.

In response to Clark's dispatches to Harrodsburg, Colonel John Bowman, Kentucky's county lieutenant, and some of the leading men from the stations rode to the Falls to confer. To prevent desertions when the nature of the expedition was finally revealed, Clark had fortified a small post on Corn Island in the river better to control his men. Here he laid out tracts for about twenty families who had accompanied the forces from Pittsburgh and the Monongahela. Clark had considered these families a nuisance but now found them useful. They would help guard whatever stores he left behind. As it turned out, they did provide a nucleus for the fortified post Clark later intended to establish on the shore.

Now it was time to explain the goal of the expedition, to justify taking men from the embattled frontiers many miles into the heart of the enemy's country. The leaders and the gentlemen from the Kentucky stations at once agreed that such an offensive would put "the salvation of Kentucky almost in their reach," though with Clark they worried about the weakness of the depleted force. After some debate among the rank-and-file, they, too, pledged to follow their officers.

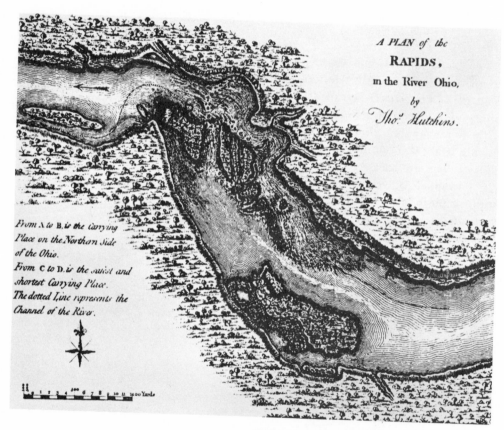

A PLAN of the

RAPIDS,

in the River Ohio,

by

Tho.ˢ Hutchins.

From A to B. is the carrying
Place on the Northern Side
of the Ohio.
From C to D. is the easiest and
shortest Carrying Place.
The dotted Line represents the
Channel of the River.

"A Plan of the Rapids, on the River Ohio" by
Thomas Hutchins, from his *A Topographical
Description of Virginia, Pennsylvania, Maryland, and North Carolina,* London 1778. This
sketch of the falls of the Ohio shows in the center foreground Corn Island where Clark established his base on his campaign to the Mississippi in 1778.

Clark found some dissidents in the ranks of the company raised by Smith. He took steps to guard against their using the boats for escape, but most of the company, under a Lieutenant Hutchings, deserted by wading the river to the Kentucky shore. Borrowing the horses of his Kentucky friends, Clark sent out men to catch the deserters, but only a few were brought back.

Colonel Bowman and Clark agreed that it was unthinkable to further strip the Kentucky stations of defenders to make up the loss. A small company of men led by Captain John Montgomery was added to the three companies Clark had brought down commanded by Helm, Joseph Bowman, and William Harrod. After spending "a day of amusement" with his friends from the Kentucky stations, Clark saw them off, "they to return to the defense of their country and we in search of new adventures. . . . "

It was now nearing the end of June. Clark had been using the time to drill his men and was satisfied of their loyalty and zeal. He had received word of the alliance with France, which encouraged the hope that the inhabitants of Kaskaskia would submit without too much opposition. It is perhaps the best measure of his qualities that though he knew his case was desperate, "the more I reflected on my weakness the more I was pleased with the enterprise. . . . "

Seven

To the Illinois Country

On the morning of 24 June, 1778, Clark's force manned its boats, shot the falls, and started down the Ohio. Clark reported a great eclipse of the sun that morning. Whether it provided an augury for success or failure, no one knew.

The little army numbered only about one hundred seventy-five men instead of the much larger force Clark had hoped for. Such a force enabled him to move more swiftly and carry less in the way of supplies, making a virtue out of necessity. Larger numbers on expeditions from Fort Pitt proved hard to control both on the march and in fighting. They were often forced to stop short of their objectives when supplies ran out. Though not by choice, Clark had surrounded himself with the kind of guerrilla band that gave him the same speed, mobility, and capacity of wide ranging that the Indians had.

Double-manning the oars and rowing day and night,

they reached the mouth of the Tennessee River in four days. Here Clark planned to leave his boats and march overland to Kaskaskia in order to avoid the spies that might be lurking along the river. Soon after the body made camp on a small island in the river mouth, a party of hunters appeared. Voicing approval of the project, a few of them joined the march. They had been at Kaskaskia recently, and so were able to give Clark useful information, both encouraging and discouraging. Clark admonished them not to speak of the possible obstacles in talking to the rest of the men. They reported that the inhabitants feared the Long Knives more than the Indians. Clark resolved "to improve upon this if I was fortunate enough to get them into my possession, as I conceived the greater the shock I could give them at first the more sensibly would they feel my lenity and become more valuable friends. . . . " It is an interesting summary of the

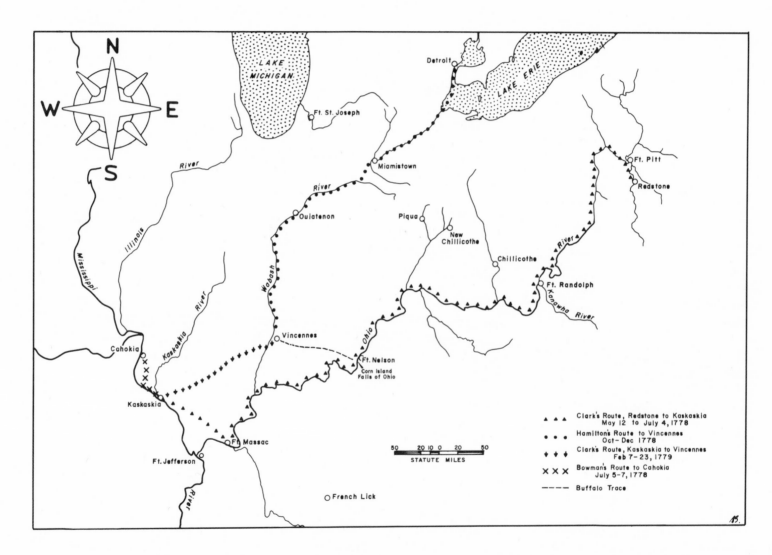

Fight for the Illinois Country, 1778-1779.

tactics Clark was to use with great success in treating with both Frenchmen and Indians.

The boats were hidden in a small stream that emptied into the Ohio near the old abandoned French Fort Massac, on the north bank of the Ohio about ten miles below the Tennessee. Shouldering their supplies, the men started the long march—about one hundred twenty miles—through swamp and brush and open prairie. The latter troubled Clark. The tall prairie grass was not yet high enough to conceal the men as the great cane brakes of Kentucky did. In "these meadows" of the Illinois country his force was in plain sight for many miles. It was a tiring journey, the officers tense for fear of discovery, the country dry, and game scarce. On the third day the guide, John Saunders, recruited from the hunting party, became bewildered and lost the trail. Clark was furious. Fearing betrayal, he grimly ordered Saunders to find the way on pain of death. The unfortunate guide finally got his bearings and the march resumed.

§ Kaskaskia Taken

After six days of marching they reached the Kaskaskia River just above the town, on the evening of 4 July. Lack of provisions during the last two days made the hungry soldiers unanimous in their fierce desire to take the town "or die in the attempt." At an isolated farmhouse, Clark surprised a family and put them under guard. Here he was relieved to learn that the town was not alerted, as the hunters had warned it was. Boats were available in ample number on the east side of the river to carry his men across.

Shortly after midnight, the little army crossed over. While part of it surrounded the town another group hurried to the fort. It was dark and unguarded, its gates open. Clark's men found Rocheblave, the commander, in bed in his quarters and made him prisoner. Soldiers ran through the streets and warned the inhabitants to stay in their houses and surrender their arms. Keeping his troops noisily circulating during the night, Clark sought to impress the citizens with his strength. He withdrew the men to the stockade at daylight so that their true numbers would not be observed.

Kaskaskia lay on the flood plain of the Mississippi River on the west bank of the Kaskaskia River five miles from its mouth under a line of bluffs that paralleled the Mississippi. It was a town of two hundred or more families, perhaps five hundred citizens in all, with an equal or larger number of Negro slaves along with some Indian slaves. Today the shifting channel of the Mississippi covers the old town. (A fort on the bluffs east of the Kaskaskia River had been abandoned before the Revolution and was not used by Clark in this period.)

Northward along the east side of the Mississippi was another French village, Prairie du Rocher, near the deserted ruins of Fort Chartres, with about a hundred citizens and nearly that number of slaves. St. Philip's, the next settlement, was an almost deserted hamlet, but farther up the river, across from St. Louis, Cahokia held three hundred or more with about eighty blacks.

The day after securing Kaskaskia, Clark sent Captain Joseph Bowman with thirty mounted men to take over these

A sketch of Kaskaskia by Philip Pittman, engraved by Kitchin, from Pittman's *The Present State of the European Settlements on the Mississippi, etc.*, London 1770. The town was on the Kaskaskia River, a few miles north of its juncture with the Mississippi. The old French fort on the eastern bluff had been abandoned. Clark captured a fort in the southeastern part of the town, formerly the Jesuit's house.

other villages, which were without defenses. A number of leading citizens accompanied him from Kaskaskia to help win over their friends. Bowman hardly stopped to rest. He had the surrender of all within three days and established his little garrison in a strong position at Cahokia.

Clark was impressed with the area he had now seized for his countrymen. Writing to his friend Mason, he said, "This you may take for granted: that it's more beautiful than any idea I could have formed of a country almost in a state of nature; everything you behold is an additional beauty; on the river you'll find the finest lands the sun ever shone on; in the high country you will find a variety of poor and rich lands with large meadows . . . varigated with groves of trees appearing like islands in the seas covered with buffaloes and other game. . . . "

Despite his success, Clark's position was still precarious. He was surrounded by "numerous nations of savages whose minds had been long poisoned by the English," he wrote Mason, with so few men he could hardly manage the "dignity that was necessary to give my orders that force that was necessary." But Clark was a master at bluffing. In his own talks with local residents (his men were instructed to do likewise), he let on that his was but a small detachment of a much larger force at the Falls. With ingenious tricks he impressed the French. He publicly proclaimed his intention of returning to the Falls, thereby cleverly getting the inhabitants themselves to plead with him to remain for their protection.

Early in the morning after taking the town, Clark met a delegation of gentlemen led by the priest, Father Pierre Gibault. Already terrified, the French were even more awed when they confronted the grimy Americans. Clark and his men had left most of their clothes by the river when they attacked. They now sat barely covered and cut by the brush and briers, altogether savage in appearance. Clark indicated that he was not ready to talk. Later, after two American traders in the village, Daniel Murray and Richard Winston, had provided a sumptuous breakfast for his hungry men, Clark relented, explained the nature of the war, told of the new Franco-American alliance, and disclaimed any intention of barbarity. He assured the leaders the town would not be plundered, women and children would not be harmed, their religion would be respected, and, indeed, all who pledged loyalty to the "Republic of Virginia" would have full freedom. The relieved people set the church bell ringing, strewed the streets with flowers, and sang in joy.

Clark's confidence that this attitude would have great weight with the Indians of the area was not misplaced. He did not seek out the Indian leaders but gave them time to hear of his strength and policies. Soon, as he hoped, they came to him expressing their wish to treat, and to learn the American side of the quarrel with Britain. In many instances the Indians were eager to realign themselves with the Big Knives who now seemed so acceptable to their French friends and were allied to their much beloved former "father," France.

Clark's character, his personal presence, his qualities

of leadership, and the confidence he always seemed to inspire now stood him in good stead. Ordinarily affable and easy with his troops, he could be stern, even severe, if occasion called for it. With French, Indians, and his own men, Clark now practiced a combination of attitudes: in turn indifferent, threatening, praising, and encouraging. All of them masked his own apprehensions. He knew it would be months before he could expect Governor Henry to hear of his exploit or send reinforcements. Meanwhile, much sooner, the British would be active to arouse their Indians against this daring intruder.

His situation was fully appreciated by the governor and his legislature when Clark's dispatches did reach Virginia. They acknowledged, "Your situation is critical. Far detached from the body of your country, placed among French, Spanish, and Indian nations strangers to our people, anxiously watching your actions and behavior and ready to receive impressions favorable or not so of our Commonwealth and its government. . . . " They professed to "feel the delicacy and difficulty of your situation. . . . " But these sympathetic responses would not reach Clark for well over six months.

Clark despaired of taking Vincennes, his final objective in the Illinois country. (Sometimes the Americans called it by different names—St. Vincent, the O Post, or Post Vincents.) It was supposed that its militia was too strong for Clark's small force. For local consumption Clark let it be known that reinforcements from the Falls would enable him to take it. Father Gibault suggested that an attack would not

be necessary, Vincennes was part of his parish—he would undertake to go with a party of villagers to win over the Wabash outpost. Accordingly, Clark sent an address to the people there carried by Dr. Jean B. Laffont while the priest went along to give the people "such hints in the spiritual way" that would assure their declaration of loyalty to the Americans. By 20 July Vincennes had pronounced its acceptance of freedom under the American flag. Captain Helm with a few men then occupied the flimsy Fort Sackville recently abandoned by the British Governor Abbott.

The period of enlistment for Clark's men had run out. Stretching his authority and exercising his powers of persuasion, Clark managed with bribes and promises to get most of them to reenlist for an additional eight months. Those who insisted on going home set off under Lieutenant William Linn. They took the captured French commander, Rocheblave, who still remained defiant, to prison in Virginia. Captain John Montgomery guarded the Frenchman and carried Clark's letters to the government.

§ **A Peaceful Period**

By autumn Virginia's new frontier on the Mississippi and the Wabash seemed to be running smoothly. Clark had established communication with Oliver Pollock in New Orleans to provide supplies and pay bills for goods and services purchased for the troops from the local French and Spanish traders. Even small armies consumed quantities of stores in a short time. They might march for a few days on dried meat—jerky—and a pouchful of parched corn, but for regular fare they had to be provided with flour, corn for cornmeal, beef, or wild game, and other food as well as drink.

To clothe the troops required coats, shirts, trousers, stockings, and underclothing, along with blankets. Hard service kept such items in short supply. Skins to make moccasins were needed as shoes quickly wore out on the march. Knives, muskets, rifles, and gunpowder were essential.

Bulky but necessary items included cooking equipment, hospital supplies, barrels for packing flour and meat, kettles for salt-making, and the salt itself for preserving meat. If pack horses accompanied an expedition or there were mounted men, fodder had also to be carried.

Costs mounted if the special services of carpenters, blacksmiths, armorers, or boatbuilders were required, as when forts had to be built or repaired, companies moved by water, or when expeditions included artillery or mounted men. Paper was in short supply and ink of poor quality, as surviving collections of records from the frontier testify, in the poorly written scraps some officers had to use in making reports.

Frontier commanders were also expected to supply the Indians with whom they treated food, drink, and ammunition. They usually wanted to offer them tobacco, whiskey, or a rum concoction called taffia to seal agreements, and they might have wished to provide colorful flags, pennants, and war paint.

Clark had dispensed with most of this on his rapid march from the Ohio, but once settled at Kaskaskia he had to contract for many such items.

§ **Indian Policy**

Most important for the safety of the Ohio and Kentucky frontiers, Clark was achieving considerable success in winning the allegiance of the Indians. He rejected the usual policy, based on fear, of lavishly distributing presents. With few presents to offer, he had little choice. He modeled his Indian policy on that of the French and Spanish, which he believed had demonstrated success. He thought it was a mistake to use soft speech with the Indians. Capitalizing on the considerable fear they already had for the Big Knives, he sought to treat them as equals and win their respect. To those who came to meet him, he bluntly offered the alternatives—lay down their arms and be friends or go to the British and fight like men.

The Indians concluded that the Virginians must be warriors or they would not dare speak that way. Boldly, Clark gave "harsh language to supply the want of men." Assuring the chiefs that the Big Knives had better principles "than what the bad birds the English had taught them to believe," Clark patiently explained the war from the American viewpoint. Many seemed to accept Clark's explanation and his broad hints that, if the British won, the oppression against which Americans were fighting would, in turn, fall on the Indians. But, he assured them, the Americans planned to

Portrayal of Clark addressing the Indians at Cahokia, from a mural by Ezra Winter in the Clark Memorial, George Rogers Clark National Historical Park, Vincennes, Indiana.

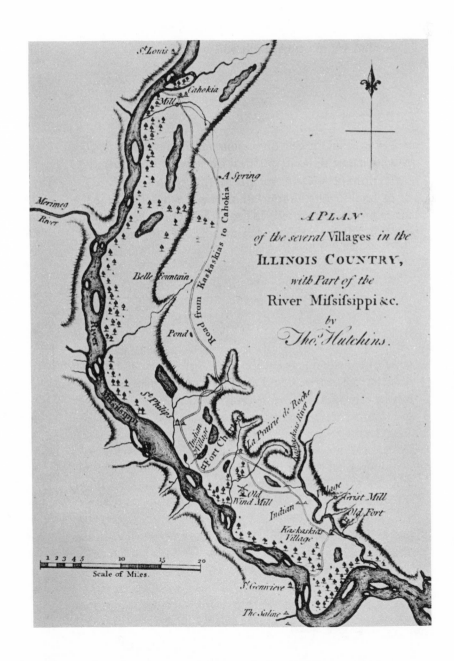

A Plan of the Several Villages in the Illinois Country, etc. by Thomas Hutchins, from his *A Topographical Description of Virginia, Pennsylvania, Maryland, and North Carolina,* London 1778. Fort Chartres (Charters) had been abandoned by the British before the American Revolution and its garrison moved to Kaskaskia.

win; the Indians would see the English "given to the dogs to eat." Those who adhered to the British cause would see their women and children suffer the same fate.

The small Kaskaskia and Peoria tribes almost immediately acknowledged friendship. Soon, Captain Bowman at Cahokia called Clark there to meet over five hundred tribesmen gathered from the Chippewa, Ottawa, Potawatomi, and Miami as well as more distant Indians belonging to the Sauk, Fox, and Winnebago. Though concerned at being in the midst of such a gathering, Clark put up a bold front, dancing the night away with his new French friends before holding the Indian council.

He had reason to be on his guard. A small party did invade his sleeping quarters in a treacherous attempt to seize him, but Clark and his guards repelled them. For a time thereafter, Clark pointedly refused to talk to the representatives of the tribe that hatched this plot. In an attempt to make amends, the cowed leader of the ostracized group produced two young braves who silently sat on the floor before Clark, their blankets over their heads, offering themselves to be tomahawked. Their stoical resignation alternated with lively curiosity as they occasionally peeked out to see what Clark would do. He had achieved his purpose and shamed the Indians. Now, much moved, he generously lifted the two men up from the floor and honored them for their bravery.

For a time, at least, Clark's astute policy deprived the British of the services of many of those with whom Clark treated. He was particularly successful with the great Black-bird, prominent among the warriors of the lower Lake Michigan region. At the Blackbird's request, Clark engaged in a lengthy discussion of the reasons for the war about which this chief, unlike most, wanted to do his own thinking.

On the Wabash, Captain Helm had equal success with the Kickapoo, Wea, Piankeshaw, and others. The Tobacco's Son, styling himself as the Grand Door to the Wabash, was particularly impressed. He became a great friend of the Big Knives, considered himself one of them, and refused to accept the blandishments of Governor Hamilton after the British recaptured Vincennes. Instead this Piankeshaw chief spent much time inside the fort in the company of the captive Helm annoying the governor and his troops.

§ **The British Retake Vincennes**

Early in August 1778, Lieutenant Governor Henry Hamilton at Detroit heard of Clark's conquests in the Illinois country. Hamilton impetuously prepared to dislodge him. Governor Frederick Haldimand had only recently arrived in Quebec to replace Carleton. Agreeing that something should be done, he left it entirely up to Hamilton. In early October, Hamilton embarked at Detroit with thirty-five Redcoats, all the post could spare, along with seventy-eight French volunteers and sixty Indians. Moving up the Maumee River to Miamistown (Fort Wayne, Indiana) Hamilton added several hundred more Indians to his force, portaged to the Wabash, and started towards Vincennes.

Clark heard of his movements, but was informed that

McIntosh, the New American commander at Fort Pitt, was moving northwest across the Ohio towards Lake Erie. Clark assumed that Hamilton had gone out to raise the Indians against General McIntosh. The soldiers at Kaskaskia celebrated Christmas strong in the belief that by this time, McIntosh had probably won Detroit.

Instead, after an arduous journey of almost two and a half months, encumbered with heavily-laden boatloads of supplies, Hamilton had descended on the luckless Helm at Vincennes. Helm's French garrison promptly deserted him; the messenger who slipped out of the fort with a hastily written note from Helm to Clark was captured before he got very far. On 17 December Helm had to surrender his undefended position and became Hamilton's prisoner.

By the first of the year, Clark guessed that the O Post had fallen, although his spies could learn nothing definite. He resolved to go to Cahokia to consult with Bowman about their defenses. Accompanied by several prominent gentlemen, a small guard, and a body of armed slaves, Clark stopped for the night at Prairie du Rocher where the residents held a ball in his honor. About midnight a messenger dashed in from Kaskaskia with the alarming news that Hamilton with eight hundred men was within three miles of that town.

Coolly calling for the dance to go on while the horses were saddled, Clark sent word to Cahokia asking Bowman to bring down reinforcements. He then rode hurriedly back to his fort. He expected to find it under siege and had equipped his men with blankets so that they could mingle with the British Indians until they found a chance to regain the stockade. Much to his relief no British had appeared.

The next few days were spent preparing for an attack. Clark wanted the townspeople to declare their neutrality if the British came. Otherwise he felt duty-bound to fight for the town with them, which would mean abandoning the fort to fight in the open. He had little hope for success if he did that. As he expected the French confessed they would not fight. Clark pretended anger. Playing out his little game with the villagers, he bound them even closer to him by treating the shamed people leniently and understandingly when the alarm proved false.

The scare had been caused by a group of Indians under white leadership sent out by Hamilton for the express purpose of seizing Clark. Some of them had watched from only a few yards away as Clark was passing on his way to Prairie du Rocher but had found his party too well armed. Scouts found their trail retiring towards Vincennes, confirming Clark's fears that Hamilton was in possession of that post. The Americans spent most of January trying to conceal from the French their apprehension about Hamilton's next move.

In Vincennes, Hamilton had found Fort Sackville neglected and rundown. He initiated strenuous efforts to repair and rebuild it, adding blockhouses at each corner, building barracks for his men, and mounting the cannon he had brought from Detroit. Of the eight hundred whites and Indians who arrived with him, most of the Indians soon

Henry Hamilton, British lieutenant governor in the West, April 7, 1775 to February 24, 1779.

Courtesy of the Harvard University Portrait Collection.

became restless and were sent off to harass the Kentucky frontier or to engage in hunting. A third of the Detroit volunteers also went home, manifesting little interest in fighting for the British.

The governor had decided that no attack on Kaskaskia was possible until spring. He was content to decrease his garrison, avoiding the expense of providing for so many. The Indians were ordered to return in time for a spring campaign against the Americans.

§ Hamilton Plans Campaign

A Spanish subject from St. Louis, Francis Vigo, had gone to Vincennes for Clark to help Helm obtain ammunition and supplies. Hamilton's men had captured him. Finally released on his promise to return directly to his home in St. Louis, Vigo complied with those terms but then hurried to his friends in Kaskaskia.

On 29 January he brought the first reliable information Clark had of what was going on. Vigo told Clark that Hamilton had sent word to all the British posts around Michigan, to the Indians of that area and to the tribes in the south, summoning them to meet on the lower Ohio in the spring for a major campaign against all the American settlements west of the Appalachians. With over a thousand men and with cannon to batter down the rude frontier forts, Hamilton planned to sweep the West clear of Britain's enemies, driving the settlers back to the seaboard. Clark's meager forces on the Mississippi would, of course, be the first to suffer.

But in the meantime, Vigo pointed out, Hamilton had only thirty Redcoats and about fifty French militia at Fort Sackville. Although the fort had been put in excellent condition, Hamilton was far from his base at Detroit. Clark knew by now that General McIntosh had not succeeded in his campaign in that direction, but it seemed unlikely that Hamilton would be receiving reinforcements from Detroit very soon. If Clark struck swiftly now, he had some chance of success. If he waited, he faced almost certain defeat when Hamilton's forces were strengthened.

The stakes were high. Clark believed that if Hamilton's plans succeeded, America would lose the West. "Our situation still appeared desperate," he recalled, "it was at this moment that I would have bound myself seven years a slave to have had five hundred troops." He was the only one in position to strike Hamilton before the British leader acquired overwhelming force. Not only Clark's own men and his conquests were threatened, but the entire American position from above Pittsburgh to south of Kentucky and back along the valleys closer to the mountains.

Who knew what reinforcements might even now be gathering around Hamilton? Even if Clark could match or exceed the numbers Hamilton had, the latter had the advantage of a strongly fortified position.

But Clark and his officers eagerly agreed that an attack on Vincennes must be attempted at once. They could count on two advantages. One was surprise. The bad weather and almost impossible trails would make such an attack appear unlikely to Hamilton. A second factor is reflected in a letter

Clark sent off to Governor Henry before he marched. "We must either quit the country or attack Mr. Hamilton. . . . Who knows what fortune will do for us? Great things have been effected by a few men well conducted. . . . " In short, daring leadership and luck might just prove to be the deter-mining factor. After all, there was no alternative. Otherwise, with reinforcements Hamilton would surely defeat him in the spring. As Clark saw it, "our cause is just and . . . our country will be grateful. . . . " If the effort failed, "this country as well as Kentucky I believe is lost. . . . "

Eight

A Few Men Well Conducted

To attack a strong fort without artillery was impossible, but it was equally impossible to drag cannon across country in the winter. Accordingly, a river boat was rigged for fighting, christened the *Willing*, and loaded with two four-pound cannon and six smaller "swivel" guns. Stocked with the extra supplies and ammunition that Clark's men could not carry, the boat started down the river under command of Lieutenant John Rogers, Clark's cousin, with between forty and fifty men. They were ordered to meet the others on the Wabash.

The next day, 5 February, 1779, Clark's force set out overland. As Clark later confessed to his friend Mason, the hardships and incredible sufferings endured by this little army surpassed almost any attempt to describe them. It is certainly a minor epic of heroic and determined men whose struggle to reach their objective surmounted unbelievable obstacles.

On the march three companies of Virginia militia under Captains Joseph Bowman, John Williams, and Edward Worthington were joined by two groups of volunteers, those from Cahokia under command of a former British officer, Richard McCarty, and men from Kaskaskia under Francis Charleville. When the French from Cahokia had ridden in with Bowman and McCarty, flags flying and drums beating, the ladies of Kaskaskia had become spirited in their support of the expedition, encouraging a similar turnout of volunteers from the lower town. In all, Clark had about one hundred seventy men, well equipped for winter weather, and accompanied by a train of pack horses to carry supplies.

Fortunately the weather was warm for the season, though it rained much of the way. A surveyor by training, Clark probably took the most direct route to Vincennes, avoiding the better marked Vincennes Trace farther north for fear that Hamilton would have scouting parties out. To keep up morale, Clark encouraged feasting and impromptu "war dances" every night. Each company in turn was provided with some of the horses to engage in hunting for the evening dinner. Rivers were in flood and the countryside overflowing. The men had to march through miles of water up to their knees or higher while Clark and his officers shouted and ran through the mud and water to encourage the troops. Even before reaching the most difficult part of the march towards the end, the force had suffered and overcome almost impossible obstacles.

Reaching the "Two Wabashes" on 13 February, they found a flood plain three or four feet deep covering an area of five miles in addition to the channels of the two rivers, the Little Wabash and, probably, the Fox. The men had to wade waist-deep following a trail, marked by the leaders, of rags tied to the brush and trees poking out of the drowned lands. A canoe was built to carry the stores across to wooden stages erected on the far side of each channel while the horses swam over. Clark and his men were amused at "a little antic drummer" who floated across on his drum. With such an obstacle behind them, there was little thought of turning back.

On 17 February they reached the Embarras River where they could hear the morning and evening guns fired at Fort Sackville only a dozen miles or so away. But the river was so high and swift and the surrounding country so flooded they could neither cross nor find a dry spot to camp. Straggling down the Embarras to where it meets the Wabash, they huddled on a small area of dry land. Wood had run out, the men were sick and discouraged, and no boats could be found

for the crossing. Fear of starvation was very real. Though the thought does not seem to have occurred to the despairing French, some of whom talked of returning, Clark and the Virginians knew that if they became really desperate they still had the horses, although they were considered too valuable to eat except as a last resort.

On 21 February the army contrived to cross the Wabash below the mouth of the Embarras. A small group of local men had been intercepted, providing one boat, and another boat was found adrift. The men from Vincennes reported that the inhabitants were inclined towards the American cause and would probably cooperate in Clark's attack.

Moving from one dry hummock to another, often forced to wade in water up to their armpits, the force consumed three days advancing the six miles or so up the east side of the Wabash towards Vincennes. The last stage of the journey was the most difficult of all. Clark kept the canoes plying through the waters to pick up those about to collapse. Exhausted men were supported by their comrades. When camp was made on such dry ground as was available, those who had collapsed were marched back and forth supported by two able-bodied men to dry and revive them. An Indian squaw paddling to town across the flooded plain with a haunch of buffalo was relieved of her burden and broth was made of it for the weakest.

§ **Vincennes Reached**

On 23 February they reached a wooded rise known as

An artist's concept of Clark's march to Vincennes, February, 1779: *"George Rogers Clark Raids Fort Sackville,"* painted by George I. Parrish, Jr., for "A History of Illinois in Paintings" and commissioned by the Illinois Bell Telephone Company.

Courtesy of Illinois Bell.

Warrior's Island. The night before they spent at a sugar camp. It had turned very cold; in the morning ice had formed on the water. But they were nearing their goal. Clark had blackened his face with gunpowder, plunged into the breast-high water with a whoop, ordered the leaders to call out when they neared dry land to encourage the others, and sternly commanded Bowman's force to bring up the rear and shoot any who faltered. His mixture of encouragement and discipline worked, and now the army was encamped in plain sight of Vincennes.

Clark sent word to the inhabitants that, if friendly, they must stay in their houses and offer no resistance. Otherwise they should go to the fort and prepare to fight. The resident who took the message had been duck-hunting on the flooded meadow when taken by Clark's men. He reported that no one was aware of the army's approach. Clark was careful not to let him see how few men were in the force.

At sunset on the twenty-third, desperate yet eager, they began their approach to the town. In full view of the populace, Clark followed a winding course. He kept the rolling land between his men and the town in such a way that only the many banners displayed by the troops could clearly be seen. He thus gave the impression that he had nearly a thousand men. As darkness fell, Clark's troops moved directly on the town. The candles had been lighted in the fort and all but the sentries had settled in for a restful evening. Some suspicion had been aroused by the swarm of people out in the streets watching Clark's advance, but his course could not be seen from the fort, and the inhabitants, when questioned, talked vaguely about watching a scouting party.

When bullets began to fly, Hamilton ordered his men to their posts. He had assumed at first that the shots were only those of a few drunken Indians. The battle raged through the dark hours. "Smart firing all night on both sides," wrote Bowman in his journal, "the cannon [in the fort] play'd smartly; not one of our men wounded, seven men in the fort badly wounded; fine sport for the sons of liberty."

After moonset Clark put men to work throwing up a trench just beyond range of the fort's cannon. Others took advantage of the fences and houses near the fort to move in so close that the cannon could not be depressed enough to fire on them. Whenever gunners appeared at the open ports, the accurate fire of the Virginians' rifles picked them off. Low on ammunition when he arrived, Clark benefited from the supplies his French well-wishers provided, dug up from the hiding places where the residents buried them when Hamilton came.

Clark could wish for the arrival of the *Willing* with supplies, reinforcements, and cannon with which to knock down the walls of the fort, but nothing had been heard from Rogers. Clark also had learned that a British reinforcement was expected so he could not afford to wait for the cannon. He must act quickly to win surrender, depending on deception and a show of confidence.

Accordingly, early the next morning, while the

Artist's portrayal of Clark attacking Fort Sackville, from a mural by Ezra Winter in the Clark Memorial, George Rogers Clark National Historical Park, Vincennes, Indiana.
Courtesy of the National Park Service.

townspeople provided the first real meal his men had enjoyed in many days, Clark sent a white flag to the fort demanding Hamilton's immediate surrender. This was refused. By noon, however, Hamilton was ready to negotiate. He suggested a three-day cease-fire, perhaps hoping for the arrival of reinforcements in the meantime. He also invited Clark into the fort for a conference. Clark declined, but proposed a meeting in front of the church, directly opposite the gates of the fort. Here the two commanders met. Hamilton was accompanied by his second-in-command, Major Jehu Hay and his captive, Captain Helm, while Clark took along Captain Bowman.

Hamilton requested terms but Clark demanded unconditional surrender. Pressed to say why he was making arrangements difficult, Clark boldly expressed a desire for more fighting, saying that his men wanted to take the fort by storm, thus ensuring them an opportunity to kill all the Indians and British partisan leaders they might find within. At this, Major Hay paled. He knew the Virginians hated him as one who had done as much as anyone to arouse the Indians against families on the frontier.

Hamilton stiffly continued to resist surrender under any but terms honorable for British officers. Yet he knew his French militia had no will to fight; they were taking every opportunity to desert him. His thirty Regulars had vowed to fight to the end, but Hamilton believed that Clark had as many as five hundred men. He had no wish for a blood bath and knew that Clark momentarily expected the arrival of cannon. The Indians promised no support. The local Piankeshaw chief, Tobacco's Son, had offered his braves to Clark,

although Clark had declined. Moments before the meeting in front of the church, the Americans had brought in a party of pro-British Indians captured as they confidently returned to the fort. On Clark's orders, four of them were crudely tomahawked and scalped right before the gate of the fort in full view of the horrified defenders. The bodies were thrown in the river. Hamilton dared not risk that fate for his men.

§ Surrender of Fort Sackville

Both Hay and Helm urged the commanders to moderate their positions. Finally, Clark ended the tense afternoon by offering more acceptable terms. Hamilton signed them. With no desire to find himself in charge of almost as many prisoners as he had men with darkness coming on, Clark set the surrender ceremony for ten the next morning. Hamilton would give up the fort, delivering himself and his men as prisoners. They would be allowed time to settle their affairs and could keep their personal belongings. On short acquaintance, Hamilton had been favorably impressesed by Clark. With no guarantees, he trusted in his captor for fair and lenient treatment.

The British marched out the morning of 25 February, 1779, and the Big Knives hurried into the fort to raise the American colors. The occasion was marred only by a powder explosion within the fort in which six were burned, including Bowman and Worthington. The accident probably contributed to the death some months later of the brave Joseph Bowman, one of Clark's strongest bulwarks, although Bowman remained active in the meantime.

Colonel Clarks Compliments to Mr.
Hamilton and begs leave to inform
him that Col. Clark will not agree
to any Other Terms than that of Mr.
Hamilton's Surrendering himself and
Garrison, Prisoners at Discretion

If Mr. Hamilton is Desirous of
a Conferance with Col. Clark he will
meet him at the Church with Capt.
Helms

Feby 24th 1779   G R Clark

George Rogers Clark demands the surrender of
British Lieutenant Governor Henry Hamilton
and his garrison at Fort Sackville, Vincennes,
February 24, 1779

Photocopy of original manuscript letter in the Draper
Manuscript Collection. Courtesy of the State Historical
Society of Wisconsin.

Now, for the first time since he had sailed from the Falls, Clark received dispatches from the governor and legislature at Williamsburg. Within two days the *Willing* arrived, its men disappointed at having missed the action. Captain Helm, with a sizable force, left immediately to intercept the expected British supplies coming down the Wabash. Near Ouiatenon, the Indian trading post, they surprised and captured seven boatloads destined for Hamilton.

The tables were turned. Not only would Hamilton not lead a great campaign against the western settlements but Clark saw the prospect of moving on to take Detroit. In the letters from Williamsburg he learned that Governor Henry promised five additional companies of militia. From letters he seized, Clark discovered that Detroit was guarded by a very small number of Regulars and the fort there was not yet completed. He had been disappointed once when the forces he originally raised were too few to go on to Detroit after taking Kaskaskia. Now, without waiting for the promised men from Virginia, he considered whether or not his forces were sufficient to take advantage of a second chance before the Indians recovered from the blow of Hamilton's surrender, also before the fort at Detroit could be finished and reinforced.

His officers were enthusiastic. French volunteers urged the attack on Detroit and promised to go, assuring Clark of a friendly reception by their compatriots in Detroit. Hamilton's French troops were given parole and allowed to return to Detroit, where their accounts of Clark's prowess led many to profess openly their American sympathies. It was said that children in the streets drank "Success to Clak [sic]" in cups of water. The returned soldiers boasted that though they had given their word not to fight against the Americans, they had not promised they would not fight for them. In a letter he sent to the Detroit commander, Captain R. B. Lernoult, by the returning French militia, Clark defiantly wrote, "I learn . . . that you were very busy making new works. I am glad to hear it, as it saves the Americans some expenses in building."

Upon sober consideration by Clark and his officers, the ambitious plan had to be deferred. Too many men were needed to guard the large number of prisoners Clark now had on his hands. Many of his men were suffering from the rigors of the march they had just endured; they were in no condition to undertake another campaign. "Never was a person more mortified than I was at this time," wrote Clark, "to see so fair an opportunity to push a victory—Detroit lost for want of a few men." Reluctantly Clark made the decision, later regretted, to delay an attack on Detroit until June or July, when he might coordinate his campaign with one by the Continental troops under General McIntosh. By then he hoped for two or three hundred Kentucky troops as well as new recruits from the inner settlements that Montgomery was supposed to bring down the Tennessee for him on Governor Henry's orders. He was assured that most of the men of the Illinois villages would join him.

On 7 March, twenty-five men led by Captain Williams and Lieutenant Rogers set off for the Falls by boat with the

The surrender of Fort Sackville, from a mural
in the Clark Memorial.
Courtesy of the National Park Service.

captive Hamilton and twenty-five prisoners. The British governor and his officers were to suffer far more at the hands of the Virginia government, convinced of their roles as "hair-buyers," than they had been prepared for by Clark's considerate treatment.

The Indians of the Wabash came to treat with Clark. Following his customary policy, he talked tough, warning that tribesmen who continued with the English would see their women and children "given to the dogs to eat," and making no secret of his plan to attack Detroit. For those who professed friendship, he set out rum and provisions, arranging a grand "frolic."

Finally, on 20 March he departed for Kaskaskia by boat with eighty men, leaving Helm in charge of civil and Indian affairs. Lieutenant Richard Brashear commanded a garrison of forty men. Captain Robert George had arrived at Kaskaskia with welcome reinforcements—George had gone to New Orleans with Willing on the *Rattletrap*.

In Kaskaskia, Clark learned that his good friend, Colonel John Todd, had been appointed county lieutenant for the new Illinois County established by the Virginia legislature. Todd's arrival would relieve the commander of responsibility for civil affairs and free him from supervision of such local militia as might serve at the Mississippi and Wabash forts while Clark was away on more distant campaigns. Such prompt establishment of county government in the regions Clark had taken was both pleasing and flattering to the commander. Commending their new "governor" to the French, he praised the villagers for their loyal and courageous support of his Vincennes campaign.

The easy surrender obtained from Hamilton was an anticlimax. It should not obscure the courage and endurance displayed in reaching that goal. Clark's achievement averted the possibility that Hamilton might have swept the West clear of American settlers—the feat assumes a major place among the campaigns of the American Revolution. By ending the British threat Clark made possible continued American settlement that really won the West.

Nine

Thrust and Parry

During the latter months of 1778 and the early months of 1779, the Americans achieved their greatest success in the West. In addition to Clark's exploits, a new commander at Fort Pitt penetrated beyond the Ohio in the north, and the settlements in Kentucky at least survived amid the continuing horrors of Indian warfare.

But until news of Clark's victories spread in the late spring of 1779, almost no letup occurred in Indian activity either on the upper Ohio or around the Kentucky stations. In Kentucky, Indians in 1777 had left grain and livestock destroyed, leading to an acute shortage of food. Men were needed to work in the fields. They were too few to keep the stockades in good repair or dig the wells that would ensure a water supply if the forts were besieged. Tools were in short supply; clothing became scarce. At night men were too tired to stand sentry. It is no wonder that in the months to come, many western outposts could neither supply men for further campaigns nor meet the state's drafts for the Continental Army.

In Kentucky, in any event, salt had to be made if game brought in by the hunters or the little available pork and beef were to be preserved for storage. Accordingly, early in 1778, while Clark was mounting his Illinois campaign, Daniel Boone led a party of thirty salt-makers from Boonesborough to the Blue Licks on the Licking River. Here, while his men boiled down the mineral waters that gushed from the springs, Boone was seized by a party of over a hundred armed and painted warriors headed for Boonesborough. He recognized that this was no ordinary array of Indians. Well-equipped, it reflected British planning and leadership. If not distracted, the Indians would shortly descend on the poorly guarded and weakened settlers. They would also wipe out the small relief party that was momentarily expected to arrive to help the salt-makers.

Boone grasped the only way out. Bargaining for good treatment, he surrendered his men. The Indians abandoned their original objectives to carry the whites back to their villages. They exhibited their great prize, Boone himself, at Detroit, although they refused to turn him over to the British. As an "honor," Boone was forced to run the gauntlet, but he escaped most of the drubbing by his fast footwork. Adopted by the great Chief Blackfish, Boone displayed a patient acceptance of his Indian life, was trusted to hunt on his own, and gained the complete confidence of the Indians.

§ New Indian Attacks

After several months, it became obvious to him that the Shawnee were again planning an attack on Boonesborough. Carefully saving powder, the parts for a rifle, and dried venison, Boone watched for his chance. One day in mid-June while he was alone with the squaws, he grabbed a horse and escaped. He rode the horse as fast as it would go until it gave out. He then proceeded on foot, stopping only once in the four days he took to cover one hundred sixty miles to shoot and roast some buffalo meat.

The word of impending attack led Boonesborough to feverish activity, repairing the fort, laying in supplies, and recruiting a few more men from the already thin forces at nearby Harrodsburg and Logan's. Two months passed without the expected attack. Working outside only under guard and penned in the cramped quarters of the stockade at night, people grew restless and tension mounted. Daringly, Boone led a small party back across the Ohio to reconnoiter the Shawnee towns. All the evidence indicated that the Indians were on the move. Boone hurried his return without making his presence known.

On 7 September his new "father," Chief Blackfish, appeared with four hundred Indians led by the senior chief, Moluntha, Chief Black Hoof, and the Chippewa leader, Blackbird. Lieutenant DeQuindre and another French partisan, Chesne (Chene), were the white leaders of this well-equipped force, and a black, Pompey, was there to help as interpreter.

At first the Indians requested a council, chiding Boone for running away from them, and urging him to return to his "family" and to bring the people of Boonesborough to live with the British. Many of the Kentuckians were already suspicious of Boone. Some who had escaped from the Shawnee had reported the apparent ease with which Boone got along with his captors. But Boone recognized the value of stalling when dealing with restless Indians. While the unarmed leaders from the fort treated in a glade nearby, people inside the stockade moved around as busily as possible to give the impression of a large body of defenders.

Both the Indians and their French-Canadian leaders appeared genial and generous in their offers of friendship. After several days of negotiation a kind of peace was arranged. The Kentuckians would not have to move away but would acknowledge British rule. Neither side was sincere. When the Indians proposed to seal the bargain with unwonted handshaking, the American representatives were suspicious but could hardly refuse. They found themselves being dragged away and on a signal the Indians opened fire. Boone and his friends broke loose, dashing for the fort and safety.

For nine days, a record for Kentucky, the Indian warriors exhibited unusual persistence in pressing the siege. Water ran low. Exhaustion and tension led to quarrels and ill-feeling within the fort. Each side hurled obscenities and insults across the pickets. With unaccustomed effort, the Indians began to tunnel under the fort. This made it necessary for the defenders to dig an intercepting countertrench. Scarce water had to be expended in dousing fires set by blazing arrows. Courageous men exposed themselves to the Indians' guns to climb up on blazing roofs to extinguish flames. The Shawnee slave, Pompey, taunted the Kentuckians from his perch at the top of a tall tree. He attempted to pick off soldiers within the fort until Daniel Boone brought him down with a well-aimed shot.

Finally, after a rainy night, the war party stole away. Their tunnel had been caved in by the downpour. Boonesborough, for the moment, was safe. The weary settlers could go back to a more normal routine and men from the other stations could return to protect their families against the lurking bands that remained after the main force retired.

§ Hostilities Between Red and White

On the upper Ohio General Lachlan McIntosh, a Regular from Georgia, took over command of Fort Pitt from General Hand in August 1778. Washington hoped that the appointment of an outsider would create easier management of the rival Virginia and Pennsylvania leaders at the post. McIntosh brought two regiments with him, under Colonels John Gibson and Daniel Brodhead. The Pennsylvania and Virginia militia were to augment this force for a major strike against Detroit.

McIntosh inherited a depleted and discouraged garrison. Desertions had mounted during the last months of Hand's command. Tory activity was evident, and the general had been forced to execute captured dissidents. Except for the Shawnee raid that took Boone, that tribe and other major tribes tributary to Detroit remained largely inactive until fall. Nearer the Ohio, the Mingo, Munsee, and some Wyandot and Huron accepted the leadership of the renegade Girty brothers and Alexander McKee. They kept up constant attacks north and east of Pittsburgh. The inner frontiers of Virginia also suffered, with attacks on the upper Kanawha, New, and Greenbrier settlements.

As Clark proceeded down the Ohio in May 1778, he stopped at Fort Randolph just after a war party of three hundred Wyandots and Hurons under Half King failed to draw that garrison out to fight. Subsequently, the Indians had moved slowly up the Kanawha in the direction of the Greenbrier. Failing to induce Clark to make a diversion, Captain McKee, commanding in Arbuckle's absence, sent two volunteers to slip past the war party to warn the inner

Boone's Fort

Fort Boonesborough, Kentucky (erected in 1775). Copied in 1903 from an original drawing by James Reeve Stuart. The drawing was owned at one time by Reuben Gold Thwaites.

settlements. The men made it, disguised as Indians with the help of Katy, the "Grenadier Squaw," who lived at Fort Randolph. This tall and imposing woman was a sister of the murdered Cornstalk, but remained friendly and offered invaluable help to the Americans on the Ohio.

Colonel Andrew Donnally was able to gather twenty-five men into his small blockhouse twenty miles from Camp Union. At sunrise, 29 May, part of Half King's force attacked. Only Philip Hammond, one of the messengers from Fort Randolph, and Dick Pointer, a slave, were awake. With the help of a barrel of water shoved against the back door of the blockhouse, the two men held off the Indians in the yard until the awakened defenders could drive them outside. This embattled little group held off the Indians until mid-afternoon, when a relief force under Samuel Lewis with Captain Arbuckle, who was returning to Fort Randolph, reached them. Soon afterward the Indians gave up the attack. Pointer was later bought by the state of Virginia and given his freedom in reward for his heroism, though he was otherwise left to live in poverty and neglect.

Many of these attacks that were falling so frequently on the frontier from the spring of 1778 until the early months of 1779 could have been avoided. The British were notably unsuccessful in persuading the Indians to undertake any large enterprise. After Clark's success they became even less so. French traders who acted as British agents in the Indian villages were wavering. After news of the alliance between France and the United States spread, they often played a double game. Charles Beaubien, whom Boone encountered

at Chillicothe, was suspected of American leanings. At the very least, he and the other French traders failed to exert themselves when the Indians appeared reluctant to fight.

But too often undisciplined soldiers and settlers, outraged at the barbarities suffered by their kinfolk and friends, committed atrocities themselves. These undid all that forest diplomats and American agents and officers were trying to do. As Helm noted a little later, "if there is not a stop put to killing Indian friends we must expect to have all foes." To eastern leaders who knew the hardship and horror of the frontier only at secondhand, the frontiersmen seemed "a wild, ungovernable race, little less savage than their tawny neighbors; and by similar barbarities have in fact provoked them to revenge," as Timothy Pickering wrote to George Washington.

§ Detroit—American Target

To Congress and General Washington, an offensive campaign against Detroit seemed the best way of ending the threat in the West. George Morgan urged it on Congress, noting that the friendly Delawares under White Eyes and Captain Pipe, with whom he had been dealing at Pittsburgh, would welcome the protection of such a force moving through their country.

Many of these Indians had accepted Christianity. Encouraged by their Moravian missionaries, David Zeisberger and John Heckewelder, the Delaware were active in trying to influence other tribes to remain at peace. Knowing that the Christian chiefs and their missionary leaders fre-

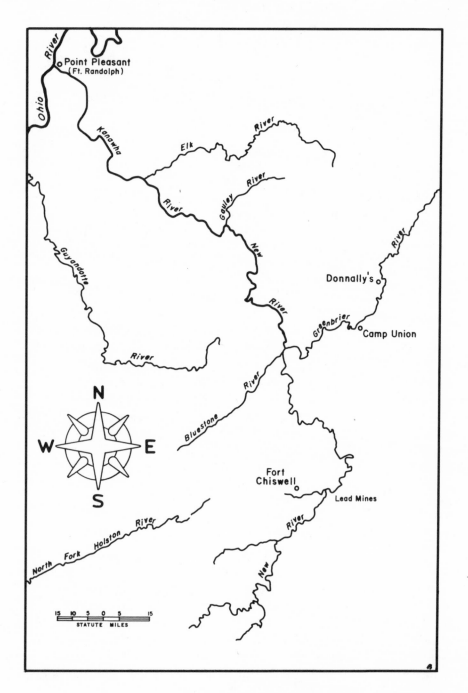

Inner Frontier, New and Greenbrier Rivers.

quently warned Americans of coming attacks, hostile neighboring tribes continually harassed the peaceful Delaware.

Morgan drew attention to the defenseless state of Detroit. As for attacks on Indian towns, he considered them useless. The villages were small and scattered, usually abandoned when strong military forces were brought against them.

Governor Henry and the Virginia Council opposed the Detroit plan. Although they favored offensive action in principle and had, accordingly, authorized Clark's expedition, they now found it impossible to promise supplies or more men from Virginia's distressed borders.

Perhaps Virginians had little expectation of claiming the Detroit area later. Maybe they coveted the honor of taking it for their own hero, Clark, rather than for the commander at Fort Pitt. Some people thought the war was almost over so such an ambitious campaign would be an unnecessary effort. They knew the British were evacuating Philadelphia, French military and naval forces were coming, and the Carlisle peace mission from Britain indicated the mother country's desire to end the war.

Congress, having ordered the attack in June, countermanded the order in July, instructing McIntosh to use what strength he had in a more limited expedition against the Indians. With over a thousand men, McIntosh had more than enough to take Detroit if he could have reached it. But maintaining an army of such size on the frontier was impossible without a line of well-stocked forts along the way.

McIntosh made a good start, building Fort McIntosh on the northwest bank of the Ohio just below the mouth of Beaver Creek, about thirty miles from Pittsburgh. Moving on, he established another post, Fort Laurens, on the west bank of the Tuscarawas River below Sandy Creek.

Presumably, the Delaware Indians welcomed this advance. They had long urged that America give them some protection against the pressure of British agents and pro-British Indians. Morgan cleared the way in a series of meetings with Delaware leaders at Fort Pitt in September 1778. Unfortunately for the future of relations with this tribe, irresponsible border ruffians killed Chief White Eyes as he traveled to join McIntosh after the treaty-making. This ruthless murder was kept secret for many years. The death was attributed to smallpox, though there were few if any cases at Pittsburgh. The loss to the American cause of the ever-faithful chief was a serious one.

General McIntosh had marched in October 1778, but had been forced to move slowly. The pack horses that were supplied proved to be in poor condition, able to carry their loads for only a few miles a day. At Fort Laurens, McIntosh was forced to stop. Food supplies ran out. The enlistments of the Virginia militia were ending. Terms of four months were not enough for a prolonged campaign and much of this time was taken up just getting to the Pittsburgh assembly point. Pennsylvania troops, enlisted by state law for only two months, had not been used at all.

No Indians at all had been encountered. Leaving a

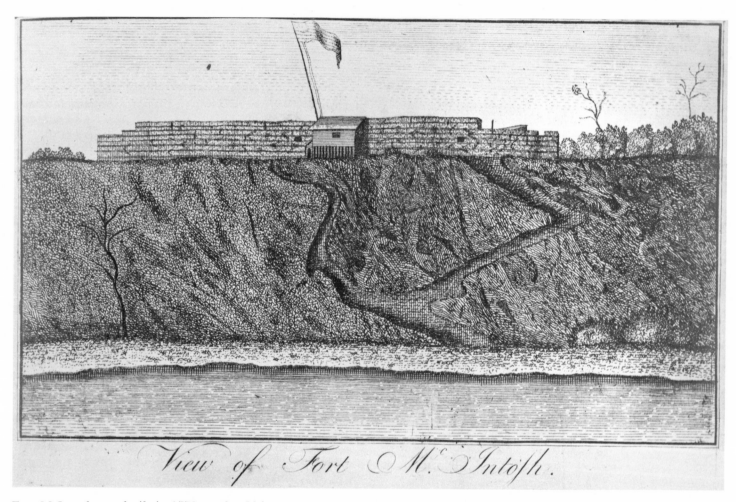

View of Fort McIntosh.

Fort McIntosh was built in 1778 on the Ohio
River west of Pittsburgh at the mouth of Beaver
River and named for General McIntosh.
From *Columbian Magazine*, January 1790. Courtesy of the
State Historical Society of Wisconsin.

garrison of one hundred fifty under Colonel Gibson, and stationing Colonel Brodhead at Fort McIntosh with his regiment, McIntosh was back in Pittsburgh well before Christmas.

Actually, Clark's little army, augmented by only a few hundred men under his kind of audacious leadership, was better suited to attacking Detroit, as he wanted to do in the spring of 1779. General McIntosh's larger army moved too slowly. Such numbers were not fitted for expeditions where distances, absence of roads, and inadequate supplies presented impossible obstacles. Food, difficult to obtain and carry for a large number of men, frequently spoiled. Ammunition was heavy, pack horses few, and forage for the animals scarce and bulky. Detroit offered a highly favorable target, had Clark's leadership been utilized or had McIntosh displayed the same kind of spirit. But gutless militia offered little chance for an advance by Clark, let alone one coordinated with the Regulars from Fort Laurens or Fort McIntosh. Distance and lack of communications played a part in disappointing such hopes.

During the winter, McIntosh maintained the garrisons at his new forts with difficulty, and kept only small detachments at Fort Hand, northeast of Pittsburgh, Fort Henry at Wheeling, and Fort Randolph at the mouth of the Kanawha. Governor Henry had been unable to replace the Virginia levies for these places because of continued attacks in Kentucky and the inner counties. Emboldened when Governor Hamilton marched to Vincennes, Indians who lurked around Fort Laurens were only partially restrained by the friendly Delaware in the region. They attacked in Westmoreland County east of Pittsburgh, along the Ohio, and up the rivers in the areas from Greenbrier to the Holston.

§ Brodhead Succeeds McIntosh

Worse, McIntosh was proving very unpopular with his officers and men. Tactless and insensitive, he also angered the local people by his disregard for their private interests. George Morgan, an ally of the Pennsylvania faction, considered his conduct ignorant, absurd, and contradictory. He was criticized for failure to take Detroit or even fight any Indians. McIntosh himself confessed that he had been brought up by the seashore and knew nothing of packhorsing in wooded country. Congress relieved him in February at his own request and Washington designated Colonel Brodhead to replace him in March 1779.

Before relinquishing command, McIntosh led a relief mission to Fort Laurens. One such supply effort had reached the fort earlier, but had been attacked by Indians under Simon Girty when leaving the stockade on the return trip. Practically the entire group of nineteen men had been tomahawked and scalped within sight of the defenders. Another group used the water route following the Muskingum River, but had to turn back because of high water. Fort Laurens lay under siege from the end of February until late March; the garrison was down to half a biscuit apiece a day for the last four days. Men chewed up old hides for whatever

A portrait of General Lachlan McIntosh (1725-1806) painted by Charles Willson Peale, c. 1781. General McIntosh commanded at Fort Pitt, August 1778 to March 1779. He was born in Scotland, and was brought to Georgia as a boy.

Courtesy of Independence National Park Collection, Philadelphia, Pennsylvania.

nourishment they could gain. The Indians had departed by the time the general arrived, but the flour he brought was lost when the pack horses bolted just as they reached the fort. Colonel Gibson and his weary men were evacuated and Major Frederick Vernon established with a fresh contingent.

When Colonel Brodhead took over, conditions at Fort Pitt were little better than they had been under Hand. Brodhead had a much larger force left him by McIntosh, but they were spread too thinly in too many small posts. Brodhead favored concentrating frontier defense at fewer strong positions, although he saw the wisdom of maintaining Fort Laurens, at least for the moment, as a deterrent against the Indians. But except for the county lieutenant, Archibald Lochry, the Westmoreland Pennsylvanians were still uncooperative even in ventures designed to relieve their own area. In addition, many of the residents of Pittsburgh were leaving to take up land around Clark's post at the Falls of the Ohio and other new Kentucky stations. Some even talked about settlement in the Illinois country.

The fortunes of the war in the West seemed to have taken a favorable turn, with Clark's success and the establishment of two spearheads north of the Ohio, Fort McIntosh and Fort Laurens. Nonetheless, the Indians became less aggressive only temporarily. A larger number of troops at Fort Pitt meant only insuperable supply problems. The Indian agent, George Morgan, resigned, charged with failures in the supply service, opposition to the policies of the Regulars, and with a hint of improper land deals.

A surge of new families taxed the diminished stores of grain, meat, salt, clothes, and shoes all through the frontier regions. Goods suitable for presents to the Indians were almost nonexistent in contrast to the lavish stores of ammunition, cloth, war paint, tobacco, and whiskey provided by the British.

Many coming west were suspected of British loyalties or efforts to escape militia duty. Many more seemed preoccupied with land deals, eager to profiteer in scarce commodities needed by the soldiers, and uninterested in anything but their own security.

§ Setbacks Require New Strategy

At the Battle of Monmouth, George Washington had failed to halt the British march back to New York. Tory and Indian attacks in upstate New York swept from Niagara as far east as the neighborhood of Albany. In March 1779, Washington made plans for a massive army under General John Sullivan to attack British and Indian strongholds on the upper Susquehanna and in the Finger Lakes region, perhaps as far as Niagara. At first Washington ordered Brodhead to gather his forces to cooperate with Sullivan's campaign. Finding that this would necessitate abandonment of Fort Laurens and would strip the Ohio frontier of defenders, Washington decided that no major offensive action should be taken in the West until Sullivan's campaign was completed.

That expedition was only a limited success. Sullivan,

with General James Clinton, moved up the Susquehanna in August 1779 with almost four thousand men, artillery, and a detachment of frontier fighters under Daniel Morgan. Just north of the Pennsylvania border at Newtown, he defeated John Butler's force of about a thousand Indians and British rangers, continuing west through the Finger Lakes. Typically, Sullivan's army was stopped short of Niagara by supply shortages and returned to Pennsylvania in October.

Meanwhile, Brodhead struggled with his problems at Fort Pitt and tried to assemble sufficient men and supplies to provide at least a diversionary strike in support of the Sullivan campaign. Since Mingos and Senecas continued to harass settlements along the Monongahela and its tributaries and in the Westmoreland area, Brodhead proposed to combine his diversion with a strike against their villages on the upper Allegheny.

With Washington's approval, Brodhead withdrew all but a few troops from Fort McIntosh and ordered Fort Laurens abandoned. Earlier, Fort Randolph had been evacuated in accordance with Brodhead's policy of concentrating troop strength. Soon afterward Indians burned it down. The weak little forts on the Allegheny were also evacuated on the grounds that Broadhead's march would cover them, but a stronger post at Kittanning, Fort Armstrong, was occupied.

On 11 August, 1779, Brodhead's army, over six hundred strong, left Pittsburgh and marched up the Allegheny. Supplies went by canoe as far as the river was navigable and were then transferred to pack horses. The advance party surprised a sizable number of warriors coming down the river, killing some and scattering the rest. Brodhead found several Seneca and Munsee towns abandoned. They were burned and crops in the fields cut down, burned, or thrown in the river. After penetrating almost to the New York line, the army returned overland, reaching Pittsburgh on 14 September.

An unknown writer who was on the march reported,

. . . we proceeded by a blind path leading to Cuscushing. thro' a country almost impassible, by reason of the stupendous heights and frightful declivities, with a continued range of craggy hills, overspread with fallen timber, thorns, and underwood, here and there an intervening valley, whose deep impenetrable gloom has always been impervious to the piercing rays of the warmest sun.*

Even if Brodhead had wished to link up with General Sullivan, he knew too little of the intervening country to do so. As it was, he had covered over four hundred miles of almost impassable mountains, timbered valleys, and overgrown country. Brodhead was satisfied that for a time Indians north and east of Pittsburgh would cause no trouble.

§ Detroit Campaign Abandoned

Preoccupied with preparations for his late summer expedition, Brodhead had not considered coordinating an attack to the northwest with Clark's hoped-for expedition against Detroit. He suggested that Clark attack the Shawnee

Frontier Retreat on the Upper Ohio 1779-1781, ed. Louise Phelps Kellogg (Madison, Wisconsin, 1917), pp. 56-57.

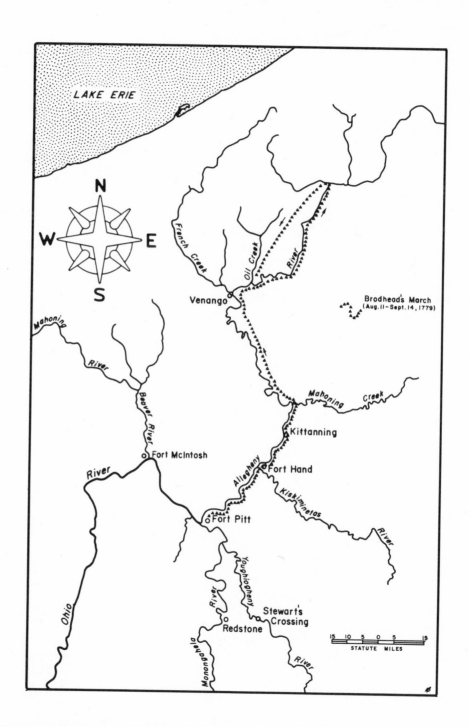

Upper Ohio, Colonel Brodhead's March, 1779.

towns but offered no assistance. Clark hoped to move against Detroit by early July 1779. Discouraged when Montgomery arrived at Kaskaskia with only one hundred fifty men of five companies Governor Henry had proposed to send, Clark next pinned his hopes on three hundred Kentucky men Colonel John Bowman had promised. He rode ahead with a party of horsemen to Vincennes at the end of June while Joseph Bowman brought the troops from the Mississippi posts after him. Montgomery brought a boatload of supplies around by water. Clark's valuable French agent, Geoffrey Linctot, took a small group of volunteers across country to Ouiatenon and back down the Wabash to Vincennes, enlisting Indian support and scouting the proposed line of march against Detroit.

To his utter disappointment, Clark found only thirty volunteers of the hundreds Colonel Bowman had promised. Bowman had gathered three hundred volunteers at the mouth of the Licking River in May. Under Captains William Harrod, Levi Todd, John Holder, and Benjamin Logan the Kentuckians had descended on the Shawnee town of Chillicothe. They killed Chief Blackfish, Boone's erstwhile "father," but retreated when word reached them that Simon Girty and a large band of reinforcements were approaching. The Shawnee pursued and attacked, killing several, but the Kentuckians got away with a large amount of plunder and over a hundred horses. At best, Bowman's invasion may have ended the threat to Fort Laurens posed by the British Captain Henry Bird from his base at Sandusky. The Shawnee and Mingo, along with the Michigan tribes, startled at Bowman's

attack and expecting Clark's campaign northward, had refused to accompany Bird.

But Bowman's raid ended any chance that Clark might be able to mount an attack on Detroit. After the fight with the Shawnee, Bowman's men refused further service and disbanded. With only three hundred fifty men at Vincennes, Clark decided he could not risk an advance, particularly since it seemed likely that General Sullivan's great army would accomplish the objective. Disposing men in garrison at Kaskaskia and Vincennes, Clark rode east along the old Buffalo Trace to the Falls where he busied himself establishing a permanent post and awaited further developments.

By the end of the summer of 1779, the tide of American advance in the West was receding. A final tragedy symbolized how easily lost was the influence that actions of the preceding year had gained.

Colonel David Rogers arrived at the Falls with a valuable cargo obtained from the Spanish. Ammunition, clothing, flour, and other necessities had been shipped to St. Louis by the Spanish at New Orleans for the use of the Americans. Empowered by Governor Henry to draw these supplies, Rogers had received releases from the authorities at New Orleans, slipped north past the British posts at Manchac and Natchez, picked up the cargo at St. Louis, and was now moving up the Ohio to deliver it at Pittsburgh.

At the falls Clark provided him with an escort of twenty-three veterans of the Illinois campaign led by Lieutenant Abraham Chapline. In all, Roger's boats carried a party of sixty or more when they left the Falls, including a few British prisoners, some passengers accepting a supposedly safe escort to Pittsburgh, and a Negro woman and two boys. On 4 October a few Indians were sighted on the riverbank ahead. Landing to attack above the Licking River (near what is now Cincinnati), Rogers fell into an ambush of over one hundred thirty Indians led by the Girtys. Only one boat escaped. Chapline and a few others were taken prisoner. Most of the party was killed and most of the valuable stores lost. Rogers died of wounds in the woods.

Now it appeared that even the line of the Ohio was not safe. The frontier was again on the defensive. Hopes for an end to the war had come to nothing. Though the British Carlisle peace mission had offered the colonists almost everything they wanted short of independence, Americans had refused to accept anything less. The British were preparing to invade the South and neither Washington nor Virginia authorities could promise the frontier more help. The British, recovering from Hamilton's surrender, were preparing anew to lead the Indians across the Ohio. The West, as 1780 approached, faced its bloodiest year yet.

Ten

The Critical Years

From 1780 on, the war in the West was a virtual stalemate. In general the reasons for this were the same for both sides: insufficient trained manpower, undependable sources of provisions, ammunition, and general supplies, and the distances and difficulties of terrain involved in getting at each other.

The British could not count on the Indians. Some tribes refused to take to the warpath after Hamilton's defeat at Vincennes. Others yielded to the overtures of the French and Spanish. Those who would fight did so unpredictably, in small, ineffective raids. When engaged in large-scale campaigns, they proved unwilling to attack strongly-held positions or broke off their efforts after trifling successes. Major attacks ended in inconclusive thrusts, striking terror into settlers, resulting in death, torture, and captivity for some, but failing to dislodge the Americans west of the mountains.

American plans to attack Detroit repeatedly failed to materialize. Retaliatory strikes against the Indians remained largely defensive in nature, failing to end Indian invasions or even to locate any large number of tribesmen for a good fight.

Special factors handicapped the war efforts of the frontiersmen. The period from 1779 to 1781 proved to be the most critical years of the Revolution in both the eastern and western theaters of the war. As the conflict dragged on, the temper of the people was tried by the seemingly endless struggle. Signs of what General Washington called loss of "virtue" appeared. Dishonesty, discontent, and the temptation to forsake the cause appeared on the increase.

In the West these took various forms — unscrupulous land speculators, men who misused public funds for private purposes, those who hoarded scarce food supplies to command higher prices, shirkers of militia duty, and deserters. Those who came west to escape taxes or militia duty could successfully resist both in an area where authorities were few and lacked the power to enforce the law. Such people justified their own behavior by denying that the state or the Congress should hold them subject to taxation or draft when they were starving, naked, homeless, with the Indians burning the very roofs over their heads.

A more troublesome faction was the Loyalists. Some who were unfriendly to the cause of independence had lived in the outposts west of the mountains from the start. Others were now joining them, chased away from their homes in the East by the hatred of their patriotic neighbors. They constituted a serious threat to the security of the frontier, always ready to inform the British of American plans, sabotage forts, disrupt defenses, and even, on occasion, to gather in sizable numbers to seize military stores or attack American troops.

Another problem afflicting the West as well as the rest of the country was the decline in value of both the Continental and the state currencies. Lacking gold or silver to back their paper bills, neither nation nor states could prevent prices for everything from rising to dizzying heights of inflation. Issuing more paper money made the situation worse. Traders and suppliers to the forces on the frontier would not accept the almost worthless paper. Soldiers, traders, and agents of foreign countries willing to provide supplies often had to be paid in land or tobacco. But even

bills drawn on such commodities found their way into the hands of speculators when the recipients, unable to use these commodities, had to sell to exploiters at a huge loss.

Clark managed to get the French and Spanish on the Mississippi and Wabash to credit him with more value for Virginia's declining currency than it brought in the East, but, ultimately, even there a silver dollar was worth fifteen to thirty times as much as the paper one, which might not be accepted at all. Depreciated money affected Indian relations as well as the supply of troops. Purchasing goods to offer the Indians as presents, to pay them for scouting and spying, or to supply their needs was next to impossible. In contrast, although the governor at Quebec complained of the great cost, the British were very generous in caring for the Indians in their service. Despite the influence his exploits had on the Indians, Clark despaired of an end to the Indian trouble as long as at Detroit, "the rule now is for them to go into the magazines [supply rooms] (when they come with a scalp or a prisoner) and take what they can carry at one load, which is the price now given for the blood of the innocent women and children on our frontiers. . . . ''

§ **More Americans Move West**

The most significant factor in determining the outcome of this struggle for the bountiful lands of the West was the ever-increasing number of Americans moving into it from east of the mountains. From conversation at Williamsburg, Clark's cousin concluded, "half [of] Virginia intended to Kentucky." Colonel Brodhead watched in amazement and irritation as a continuous stream of people passed through Pittsburgh on their way down the Ohio to the Falls and other Kentucky stations. Not only were they coming in the expectation that Clark had made the new lands safe but in their numbers they were providing forces that would seem to guarantee that safety. Sheltered or exposed, they had come to stay. Their presence would do more to win the West, in the end, than the particular victories or defeats of the small guerrilla bands that fought for either side. Win or lose, these small engagements did not permanently discourage those who settled. By the end of 1780, from ten to twenty thousand settlers made up the growing population of Kentucky.

Yet in their increasing numbers and in the nature of those who came, a new kind of weakness was created. Scattered widely in new stations and even in isolated cabins and farmsteads, they were exposed to Indian attacks. Militia officers found it impossible either to defend them or to call them together quickly when attacks loomed. They were too many to gather into a few strong forts, where provisions simply would not have been available to feed them. Apart from those new arrivals who were not sympathetic to the American cause, many were so obsessed with the fever for land that they were heedless of the consequences of exposing themselves. Some borderers even attempted settlement across the Ohio in Indian country, jeopardizing the uneasy peace with nearer tribes hard won at the conference table. The commander at Fort Pitt repeatedly had to send troops to drive

such settlers back. Some of the newcomers as well as many of the older settlers were so intent on acquiring land and such inveterate Indian-haters that they were guilty of repeated irresponsible criminal acts towards even the most peaceful Indians.

§ **Advance on the Cumberland**

The spring and summer of 1780 saw settlement extended westward in the Tennessee region as well as on the upper Ohio and in Kentucky. Families from the southwest corner of Virginia and the North Carolina frontier had been edging down the Holston and into the farther valleys of the French Broad and Tennessee rivers since the defeat of the Cherokee in 1776. In the fall of 1779 that tireless colonizer Judge Richard Henderson directed the settlement of a new area in middle Tennessee on the Cumberland. Having lost his bid for a proposed new colony, Transylvania, on the Kentucky River, he had accepted lands along the Green River farther west in compensation. Now he sought to develop another part of the area he believed he had bought from the Cherokee.

His agent was James Robertson. Ever since Lord Dunmore's War, Robertson had been an active civil and military leader in the Southwest. He had served as agent in continuing efforts to keep the Cherokee peaceful and fought along with men like John Sevier, Evan Shelby, and William Campbell when the irreconcilable Dragging Canoe and his Chickamaugas attacked. During the winter of 1778-1779

Robertson blazed a trail overland to the great bend of the Cumberland to view the site of prospective settlement at French Lick (now Nashville, Tennessee). From there he made his way to the Ohio and up the Wabash to Vincennes to confer with George Rogers Clark. Clark had bought claims to many acres of land on the Cumberland awarded by Virginia to veterans of the French and Indian War. Robertson wanted to clear up rights to this land. He probably succeeded in convincing Clark that the area lay within the soon-to-be-determined boundaries of North Carolina and therefore Clark's Virginia land grants were worthless.

In late fall of 1779, Robertson set out with a number of the men who proposed to locate in the new area. With their hired men and slaves they drove their stock overland to French Lick on the Cumberland. Burly John Donelson guided the women, children, and additional families and their slaves by boat down the Tennessee and up the Ohio and Cumberland to the new settlement. They arrived in late April 1780. Here these families from the Holston, Watauga, Nolichucky, and Clinch valleys, and from farther east in Virginia and North Carolina, established eight stations, Nashborough and Eaton's being the largest.

Under Henderson's direction they drafted land laws, the "Cumberland Compact" adopted on 1 May. In the following years of the war, few joined the original three hundred or so settlers. The Chickamauga, aided by renegade and wandering tribesmen from the Chickasaw, Creek, and Choctaw nations, kept them constantly in danger. Many were killed, some moved down river to the Spanish settlements, and others died of disease. That these exposed middle Tennessee posts survived was testimony to the steadfast leadership of James Robertson.

§ **Trouble with Loyalists**

In these later years of the war, the problem of the Loyalists, which had troubled the established eastern communities from the start, beset the frontier as well. Colonel Brodhead reviewed the influx of people arriving along the Ohio during the summer of 1780 and concluded that all too many of them were not seriously interested in the new nation. Events of the summer provided evidence that some would willingly go over to the British rather than withstand attack. By September, Brodhead had to suppress a potential Tory uprising right at Fort Pitt itself.

The same sort of trouble loomed at the interior settlements in southwestern Virginia. Here it constituted a serious threat not only to the settlers of the area but to the entire United States, for near the New River were the lead mines around Fort Chiswell on which all the armies of the new nation depended for ammunition. Colonel William Preston, county lieutenant, acted vigorously to suppress a Loyalist group in the summer of 1779. Then a force of one hundred thirty men headed by Colonel William Campbell and Major Walter Crockett broke up a nest of plotters, reporting, "shot one, hanged one, and whipped several."

The Tories became even more troublesome in 1780 when the British, invading the South, urged them to declare themselves and form new British militia companies. Colonel

Preston set guards over the lead mines, arrested known Tory leaders, and, at Jefferson's suggestion, considered calling for George Rogers Clark. In June a force of two hundred Loyalists gathered secretly near Fort Chiswell. Only the fortunate chance that a company on its way to reinforce Clark at the Falls was camped nearby frustrated the Loyalist plan. Colonel William Campbell's militia routed another group plotting to seize the mines in July. Prompt, often harsh, treatment by enraged patriots prevented serious consequences from these intrigues of unwilling "Americans."

The defeat of the British at the Battle of King's Mountain helped to put an end to the Loyalist threat. Major Patrick Ferguson at the head of a thousand Loyalist troops had penetrated into Western North Carolina as part of Cornwallis's southern campaign. The aroused frontiersmen turned out: Colonel John Sevier, Colonels Isaac Shelby and William Campbell of Virginia, and Colonels Benjamin Cleveland and Charles McDowell of North Carolina, joined at Cowpens by Colonels James Williams and William Graham, gathering a total force of some fourteen hundred men. On 7 October, 1780, they trapped Ferguson on the top of King's Mountain. Giving no quarter, the Americans fought without concealing the fury they felt at atrocities committed by such Loyalist bands. Ferguson was shot out of his saddle and lay dead on the ground with one foot still in his stirrup. Others could surrender only with difficulty. American commanders had to struggle to stop their men from firing.

After this, those in the West whose sympathies lay with the British could do little but submit to the local authorities, though they often furtively avoided military service or withheld supplies while they circulated unfounded rumors detrimental to the patriot cause.

Migration to the southwest frontiers from 1779 onward brought renewed trouble from the Cherokee as well as from Loyalists. Evan Shelby and John Sevier with nine hundred militiamen attacked and burned eleven towns of the hostile Chickamauga faction and upper Creek Indians in the spring of 1779 when the Indians rose to support the British campaign. Georgia and Carolina militia kept up the pressure in 1780 and 1781 by systematic invasions of the middle and lower Cherokee country when the British tried to arouse them against the Americans. The Cherokee had seemed thoroughly cowed by their initial defeats at the beginning of the war. However, because of the continual movement of settlers into the Indian lands in the intervening years, they occasionally made trouble until their final submission in 1782.

§ War Continues

While persistent immigration posed new problems for the West, the frontier war went on. Clark had disposed his men as strategically as possible in the fall of 1779. Exercising overall command from the Falls (Louisville), he had Lieutenant Colonel Montgomery, his second-in-command, at Kaskaskia, with garrisons at Cahokia under McCarty and at Vincennes under Captain Thomas Quirk. Still hopeful that he could march against Detroit next season, Clark was far from the idle during the winter.

Thomas Jefferson (1743-1826), governor of Virginia, June 1779 to June 1781. Jefferson is the central figure in this detail from John Trumbull's painting, *The Declaration of Independence*.

Courtesy of Yale University Art Gallery.

At the request of the new governor, Thomas Jefferson, who had succeeded Patrick Henry in the summer of 1779, Clark began plans for a new fort on the Mississippi at the mouth of the Ohio. He sent Captain James Shelby with thirty men and some French militia to the important trading station on the upper Wabash, Ouiatenon, where Shelby and Clark's Indian agent, Linctot, exerted their influence to win the numerous tribes that traded there. With some two hundred fifty Indians and militia, Shelby planned to attack the small British post at St. Joseph on the St. Joseph River about twenty miles inland from Lake Michigan, to destroy the fort and seize its stores. However, his volunteers refused to march for lack of shoes.

Clark lost an invaluable officer when the brave Major Joseph Bowman died in August 1779. He was also soon to lose the help of John Todd, who was asking to be removed from the post of county lieutenant of Illinois at Kaskaskia. Todd was uncomfortable dealing with the French-speaking inhabitants and found himself unsuited to the rigors of life in such an advanced frontier.

But Clark had acquired the services of able new men, like Shelby and Quirk, who rose to replace his original company commanders, and newcomers like Robert George, who resigned his Navy commission to accept a captaincy in the Virginia militia. George shortly became the commander of the new Fort Jefferson at the mouth of the Ohio. Now, too, there was another Clark on the frontier. Nineteen-year-old Richard Clark, a younger brother to George Rogers Clark, arrived at Kaskaskia in the summer of 1779. Clark made

"Dicky" a lieutenant, vowing to his father, "If I can get him to embrace the air of an officer I don't doubt but he may make a good appearance in a short time."

At Fort Pitt the ambitious Colonel Brodhead, like Clark, had high hopes of winning laurels by a successful attack on Detroit. Unlike Clark, of whom he became increasingly jealous, Brodhead as commander of Regulars could act only under orders from George Washington, the commander-in-chief. Clark, holding a Virginia militia commission, was subject to the orders of the state government. The easy-going Governor Jefferson left him free to attempt anything his resources permitted.

Washington concluded in the fall of 1779 that an attack on Detroit was out of the question for that season or the winter. Brodhead, plagued by continued discord between Virginians and Pennsylvanians, weakened by Loyalist malcontents in his district, and by the movement of many men down-river to Kentucky, had neither enough men nor supplies. Frustrated in his efforts to gather men for enterprises like the expeditions that had brought fame to Clark, Brodhead could not even find men to replace the militia whose terms were expiring. He had to abandon his forts on the Allegheny and had difficulty manning those on the Ohio.

Notwithstanding the present limitations, Washington urged Brodhead to continue preparations for a future offensive against the British. A new factor had entered the equation. Colonel Arent Schuyler De Peyster formerly British commander at Mackinac, had taken over at Detroit and energized the British, speeding their recovery from Hamil-

Colonel Daniel Brodhead (1736-1809), commander at Fort Pitt, April 1779 to September
1781. Colonel Brodhead was born in New
York, and was a resident of Reading, Pennsylvania, at the outbreak of the Revolution.
From a daguerreotype copy of a miniature in
the collection of the State Historical Society of
Wisconsin.

Courtesy of the State Historical Society of Wisconsin.

ton's loss and infusing new spirit into the wavering Indians. To keep in touch with developments in the enemy camp, Brodhead asked for a French agent. He was gratified by the arrival in the summer of 1780 of Colonel Augustin Mottin de la Balme, a friend of Lafayette. De la Balme, with the already active Linctot, appeared ready to use his influence to keep the Indians out of the British interest.

§ Problems with the French

During the summer while Linctot labored to keep the Delaware quiet, de la Balme proceeded to Vincennes and Kaskaskia. The French residents of the Illinois country were becoming increasingly disenchanted with the Americans. Virginia's treasury was empty. As a result, bills owed to the French for supplies were not paid. Bills drawn on Pollock, Virginia's unofficial agent in New Orleans, were similarly treated. Pollock, though he kept trying, had practically exhausted his credit and his personal resources in buying supplies for the Mississippi and Wabash posts. Virginia and Continental money circulating in the Illinois area was by now almost worthless. Clark's commander at Kaskaskia, Colonel Montgomery, further alienated the residents. Driven to desperation, he had to seize by force cattle, grain, and other supplies his troops needed.

Consequently, the French inhabitants resolved to win their freedom for themselves. They applied for aid to the French envoy in Philadelphia, La Luzerne, offering to enlist a thousand men and two thousand Indians. When de la Balme arrived, they hailed him as their chosen instrument.

De la Balme laid his plans, spurning all help from Clark's men. Of course the indolent French residents did not perform as promised; he raised fewer than a hundred men. Notwithstanding this and counting perhaps on Indian recruits and an uprising of the French at Detroit, he set out in October 1780. Moving up the Wabash, he crossed to Miamistown, the important British trading post at the head of the Maumee. After waiting for over a week for reinforcements, his small band plundered the British trading houses. The Indians of the area, enraged at the loss of their goods, fell upon the little army that very night, killing de la Balme and most of his men.

So another attempt to approach the prized Detroit failed. DePeyster was chagrined that the French had come so far without his learning of it. He suspected that de la Balme might well have caused considerable trouble at Detroit if he had not aroused the wrath of the Indians. DePeyster had little faith in the constancy of his French subjects, of whom his predecessor had complained, "all the Canadians are rebels, to a man."

The French effort ended on a minor note with the failure of a small group de la Balme had sent out against Fort St. Joseph. Sixteen men from Cahokia led by Jean Baptiste Hamelin raided that post in early December, capturing a quantity of goods. But Indians under Lieutenant DeQuindre overtook them and inflicted much the same fate as had befallen de la Balme—four killed, two wounded, and seven captured.

These failures did not end the growing resistance of

the inhabitants of the Illinois country. Methods employed by Richard Winston, who followed Todd as county lieutenant, and by Clark's officers in their efforts to support themselves, continued to anger the French. Even Clark's most loyal friends in the Illinois, men like Linctot, Major François Bosseron, and Jean Marie Philippe LeGras, signed repeated complaints.

Soldiers quartered among a civilian population always create problems. Recurrent shortages aggravated the strain as the populace was forced to share its meager resources with invaders. The Americans' claim that they came as liberators was often belied by their ill-concealed enthusiasm for fur trade profits and land speculation. French villagers feared for their property, their Catholic religion, and their very way of life in the event the United States made good the tenuous hold it had on the Illinois country.

Whatever Clark had done with fairness and diplomacy to dispel French suspicion and win the allegiance of these inhabitants was often nullified by tactless, sometimes ruthless treatment at the hands of lesser men left in control. From the American viewpoint, little could be done. Even Clark had to keep the requirements of military security uppermost. Since Virginia could not feed and supply the feeble garrisons he had left in the Illinois country, they had to extract their needs from the inhabitants, by force if necessary. Some of Clark's subordinates were doubtless corrupt and self-seeking.

Nevertheless, observers as different as Father Gibault and British Lieutenant Governor Hamilton found the French lethargic, undisciplined, and dissolute. Given the cultural gap between the villagers and Virginia's Big Knives, each was likely to exasperate the other. In wartime, allies not infrequently make uneasy partners.

Eleven

Sagging Defenses

In the West, America both gained and lost when Spain entered the war against Britain in April 1779. Governor Bernardo de Galvez at New Orleans acted swiftly and brilliantly, capturing the British posts on the lower Mississippi, Fort Manchac and Baton Rouge, and taking the surrender of Natchez, all in the summer of 1779. The following year he mounted a successful attack on Mobile and deprived the British of Pensacola in 1781.

Therefore, the southern Indians were receiving no help from the British posts on the east bank of the river and supplies for the Americans could flow more freely up the Mississippi from New Orleans—had there been money to purchase them. But it did deprive both Clark and Brodhead of British targets, Manchac and Natchez, that they had considered as alternatives to Detroit.

Spain, although it was helping the United States, did so in furtherance of its own hostility towards the British. It did not favor independence for America nor did it become an ally of the United States when it entered the war. Not only did it refuse to offer Americans the right to navigate the Mississippi if they won their independence, but also Spain harbored designs on land east of the Mississippi as far as the Ohio. It would utilize a thrust of its own, late in the war, to justify claiming even more of the Northwest. For Americans who were enduring cruel hardships to win their new homes west of the mountains and for whom the Mississippi was a vital outlet for exports too bulky to ship back through the mountains, Spanish activity was a mixed blessing.

§ **Indian Attacks Resume**

The winter of 1779-1780 was unduly severe. Ice and snow covered everything from the Great Lakes to southwestern Virginia. Game became scarce, cattle died, and food supplies dwindled. But winter did keep the Indians at home.

In early spring, the raids began again. Lochry reported Westmoreland County attacked in four places in April. Indians struck the region of the Clinch, Holston, and New rivers. They lurked around Boonesborough in March, killing the prominent early settler, Colonel Richard Callaway, and others. A day-long fight at Bryan's Station on the Elkhorn left one man killed, horses stolen, and cattle slaughtered. The increased number of settlers were too scattered to help and only provided defenseless, attractive targets for the warriors.

Clark was beset with calls for help. Cahokia feared attack and required him. Colonel Preston might want him to put down the Tories. The Kentuckians favored an offensive against the Shawnee, repeating what they had earlier told Clark, "You are the man a majority of Kentucky militia would choose to command them." But Clark, preparing to leave for the mouth of the Ohio in April to supervise construction of a new fort, dismissed these claims. A limited venture against the Shawnee would not help. The Indians would be hard to locate and bring to battle. He was dreaming again of the larger goal, planning to take Detroit during the summer. An attack on the Indians would only dissipate his strength.

Further, both Clark and Brodhead were hearing rumors of a projected major British campaign. These were accurate. From his post at Mackinac the British commander, Patrick Sinclair, was preparing an expedition against both Spanish and French posts on the Mississippi. Led by a trader, Emanuel Hesse, a mixed force of Indians, servants, and traders collected at Prairie du Chien on the Mississippi. To the west the loyal Sioux were called on. Along the river tribesmen from the Sauk, Fox, Menominee, Winnebago, and Ottawa nations were attracted by the chance to strike at traditional enemies, the Indians of the Illinois country.

An urgent appeal from Cahokia followed by dispatches from Colonel Montgomery at Kaskaskia and the Spanish commandant at St. Louis, Fernando De Leyba, summoned Clark from the construction of Fort Jefferson. Now Clark could repay the staunch support and many kindnesses De Leyba had furnished during the uneasy period when Clark first held the Illinois towns. De Leyba and Clark had become warm friends. Clark's friendship with the commandant's niece provides the only known hint in Clark's career of a romance, though it came to nothing.

Clark hurried up the Mississippi, arriving with a small detachment to take command at Cahokia just a day before Hesse, with nearly a thousand men, struck on 26 May. After a skirmish there, Hesse diverted the main attack to St. Louis. There, De Leyba met the enemy. Vigorous fire, supported by cannon, and the heroic efforts of reinforcements from Ste. Genevieve soon discouraged the motley British force. Taking their vengeance on a nearby undefended town and straggling homesteads, the British killed about seventy and captured others before they withdrew. Colonel Montgomery with three hundred fifty Virginia, French, and Spanish troops was ordered to pursue but accomplished little beyond burning Indian villages up the Illinois and Rock rivers.

Meanwhile the second section of the British offensive got under way. DePeyster sent Captain Henry Bird from Detroit with about one hundred fifty Regulars and French militia and as many as a thousand Indians against the Falls of the Ohio. Well-armed bringing artillery to batter down the Kentucky forts, Bird moved along the Maumee and down the Miami River to the Ohio early in May.

Warning of the attack came to Kentucky from Lieutenant Abraham Chapline in late May. Chapline, captured in the defeat of David Rogers on the Ohio in the fall of 1779, had escaped from the Sandusky Indian villages along with George Hendricks, earlier captured with Boone at Blue Licks. Upon receiving the alert, Colonel John Bowman hardly knew where to turn. Clark was back at Fort Jefferson again. His absence, known to the British, had probably encouraged their thrust. Brodhead could offer no help from the upper Ohio since Bird might turn against him. Colonel Arthur Campbell tried to send help from the interior counties but those troops were detained by the Loyalist uprisings and the attacks of Dragging Canoe.

Bird's force unaccountably turned away from an attack on the Falls. His Indians may have feared the return of Clark, or Bird may have heard of reinforcements coming from Virginia. Moving up the Licking River, he attacked two small posts, Ruddle's and Martin's. The settlers could not have withstood his cannon and anyway they showed little disposition to fight. Several hundred surrendered and will-ingly agreed to go to Detroit. Mostly Germans, they probably had never been strong in the American cause. Unfortunately Bird was unable to control his warriors. Only a portion of those captured arrived as prisoners at Detroit in August.

Clark had learned of Bird's approach. With two companions, he struck out overland from Fort Jefferson, reaching Harrodsburg just before word arrived of the attack on the Licking. It was too late to prevent that disaster. Now the question was how to prevent the British from carrying out another attack. Minds were divided. At Pittsburgh, Brodhead contemplated small, rapid mounted attacks across the Ohio, but had to postpone them month after month for lack of men and supplies. In July, General Washington ended whatever hope Brodhead may have had for a major campaign, announcing flatly that no Regulars could be spared and warning Brodhead against placing any faith in militia.

The Virginia government advocated several new forts along the Ohio River, but could provide no additional men. All they had were required to meet the British invasion of the Carolinas. Clark had to take the garrison from Vincennes to man Fort Jefferson and even with that encountered great difficulty in building the new outpost up to strength. He saw no possibility of maintaining additional forts.

§ Clark Leads Attack Against Shawnee

Reluctant though he was to squander his resources on a strike against the Indian towns, Clark had to bow to the

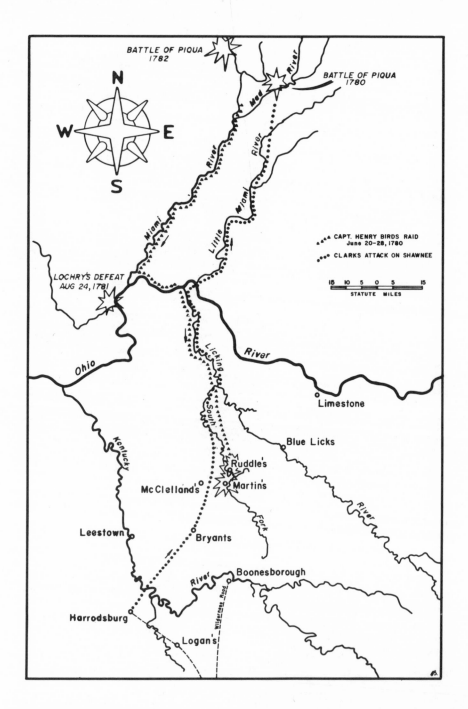

Kentucky Frontier, 1780-1782.

urging of Kentucky leaders and do that. On 1 August, 1780, a thousand men from Kentucky crossed the Ohio near the Licking and moved north towards the Shawnee towns. Clark led Benjamin Logan, James Harrod, Levi Todd, Daniel Boone, William McAfee, and many other veterans of the West in vengeance for their years of suffering. This time Clark, like Bird, had some small artillery pieces. Chillicothe was empty and partially burned. The Indians had departed so hastily that corn and snap beans were still boiling on the fires. The men enjoyed the addition of roasting ears and green beans to their marching fare of parched corn.

The next day they cut down and burned the cornfields, reserving only a few acres to provide roasting ears for their return trip. The force then turned towards Piqua, between the Miami and Little Miami rivers. Shawnee spies were detected moving ahead of them, obviously drawing them to a fighting ground of the Indians' choice. On the evening of 8 August Clark's troops came within sight of the Indian town. Women and children had fled; the warriors were prepared to make a stand. Savage fighting broke out at once in the fields around the village. Forced back, the Indians concentrated in their fort, which was promptly knocked apart by the Kentuckians' light cannon. By the time darkness fell the three hundred or so Shawnee, Mingo, Wyandot, and Delaware warriors with the notorious Girty brothers had been routed. Thirty or forty Indians lay dead; the rest escaped. Clark lost about fourteen men.

In the midst of the battle, a white prisoner had tried to escape his Indian captors but was mortally wounded. He was Clark's cousin, Joseph Rogers, who had been captured almost four years before in December 1776 while trying to recover the powder Clark and Jones had been conveying to Kentucky. Identifying himself to nearby soldiers, Rogers called for his cousin. Clark rode up, obviously deeply affected, but with his usual strong control was heard to say only that he should have thought Rogers might have escaped to the oncoming Kentuckians sooner.

Clark was much tempted to go on to Detroit. He knew the post had only two hundred defenders. The hot August weather, uncertainties about food supplies, and the reluctance of the Kentuckians who had left their stations almost undefended prevented this move. By the latter part of August, Clark was back at Louisville, the name now given to the settlement at the Falls.

§ **Detroit Plan Abandoned**

Whatever hopes Clark still nourished for his Detroit campaign gradually died. He alienated some possible supporters by refusing to countenance a plot to separate the West from both Virginia and Pennsylvania. These "separate state" enthusiasts would continue to provide interference to the plans of both Clark in Kentucky and Brodhead at Fort Pitt.

Jefferson killed any hope for a major campaign in 1780 when he informed Clark in September that Virginia had no money for a large-scale expedition. He was sending Colonel Crockett to Clark with, if possible, about two hundred eighty men. He would try to arrange a dependable supply service from the inner counties for the frontier. But this was all Virginia could do for the West in view of the demands of the southern armies.

The plight of Fort Jefferson also demanded Clark's attention. Captain Robert George had been under siege almost all summer. Colonel Montgomery brought a few men and Indians in relief just as the siege ended. Only with difficulty could he persuade George to maintain the garrison there. Too few families had settled in the vicinity to provide the fort with food. Prices of goods from New Orleans were exorbitant, and the only people not deserting both town and fort were those who had no horses to ride or no energy to row back upstream. Many had fled down the Mississippi taking the government-issued supplies with them. Many who remained were starving and dying. Private traders and the public supplier, John Dodge, were profiteering. The fort had been placed on the banks of one of the Mississippi's inner channels, leaving the fort too far from the main channel to be easily supplied.

All in all, Clark was so busy that, as he wrote his father, he had given up all attempts at locating land claims for himself, his family, and his friends. Indeed, he had become so incensed about the neglect shown by some settlers to his recruiting efforts for the Shawnee strike that he had high-handedly closed the land office to divert the people from their feverish pursuit of claims.

In late fall, leaving Colonel George Slaughter in command at Louisville, he returned to Virginia to spend Christmas with his parents.

At Fort Pitt, Brodhead fought frustration and was fighting with many of his officers as well. His abusive treatment of Pennsylvania militia captains and county lieutenants brought him a rebuke from President Joseph Reed of Pennsylvania. Captains of the Ohio and Allegheny forts often responded too slowly to his brusque orders and felt his displeasure.

He planned an attack on the Indians in northeast Ohio in May. Short of artillery and supplies, he postponed it to June. In July it was scheduled for August. But low water in the rivers prevented mills from grinding corn so provisions became even more scanty. Faced with constant desertions, Brodhead was forced to appeal to Clark to stop men fleeing down the Ohio. In September he called on the surrounding counties to have militia ready for an October attack on the Indians. He began to fear that his inaction would lose him his reputation. Finally, in mid-October, he withdrew the garrison from Fort Henry at Wheeling and gave up his plans.

Mingo, Wyandot, Munsee, and some Delaware and Shawnee continued to kill, burn, and capture. People in Westmoreland County "forted up," men at Fort McIntosh ambushed several Indians, but only after they had killed some nearby field workers. Settlers back along the Monongahela and Cheat who had believed themselves safe learned otherwise. Brodhead could only rave at these "hellhounds of the forest" and wish he had the means to fight back.

§ Jefferson Orders Attack on Detroit

During the summer of 1780 the Virginia government

moved from Williamsburg to Richmond. Here, towards the end of the year, Clark met with Governor Jefferson. On Christmas Day, the amiable but unrealistic governor issued ambitious orders to his western commander. His logic was sound, but his means were no more adequate than they had been and were shortly to become much less so. He called for an expedition of two thousand men against Detroit. Following Clark's reasoning, he argued that, by putting the British on the defensive, the United States would not face an invasion from the West at the same time the British were approaching from the South.

George Rogers Clark was to command this effort, almost wholly a Virginia enterprise. Elaborate plans to provide a supply line were proposed. Provision was made for maintaining the existing frontier forts. The army would approach Detroit by traveling up the Wabash as soon as the ice was out of the stream in the spring but before the ice cleared from Lake Erie, ensuring that the British would get no help from their little flotilla of gunboats. Clark was given complete authority, even to the extent of changing his objective if the main target proved unattainable. General Washington gave enthusiastic approval by mid-January.

By that time events made the whole proposal even more visionary than at first. The American traitor, Benedict Arnold, now a brigadier general in the British service, landed near Richmond at the head of twelve hundred Loyalist troops from Canada, New York, and Pennsylvania on 3 January, 1781. Clark was pressed into service with Steuben's outnumbered Regulars. He distinguished himself beyond the achievements of most of the American defenders. Nevertheless, Arnold took Richmond, plundering and burning supplies and tobacco—the latter the most valuable to the Americans as an article of exchange for European war supplies.

Clark was detached from Steuben's command to take up his western project by the middle of January. By this time Arnold had gone into winter quarters at Portsmouth. General William Phillips assumed command of the British forces in Virginia in March, and by May Cornwallis had arrived to take over. The Virginia government moved to Charlottesville, but Cornwallis's brilliant cavalry commander, Lieutenant Colonel Banastre Tarleton, chased Jefferson into the mountains when he attacked there in June. Some members of the legislature were captured; the rest unceremoniously rose from their deliberations and fled. Virginia faced a critical situation in the spring and summer of 1781. Large numbers of Virginia men had already been drawn from the state to help General Greene farther south. Thus the likelihood that Clark could assemble the requisite number to take Detroit appeared wildly improbable.

Before he left Richmond, Clark requested a Continental commission. As a militia colonel, he would otherwise find himself junior to Colonel Brodhead, who held his rank as a Regular. Congress refused his request. Instead, Governor Jefferson appointed Clark a brigadier general for the campaign.

Informed by both Washington and Jefferson of Clark's mission, Brodhead fumed. The glory would go to Clark while Brodhead was consigned to a defensive role.

With increasingly ill-concealed hostility, he maintained only cold and correct relations with Clark. It only made matters worse when Jefferson requested Brodhead's best officer, Colonel John Gibson, and his entire regiment for Clark. In addition, Washington approved attaching a Regular artillery company from Fort Pitt to Clark's force. Brodhead complained about his own lack of money to buy provisions for his men while Virginia was buying up everything available for Clark's expedition. The final blow came with orders from Washington reducing the number of Regulars on the upper Ohio. Washington desperately needed men and probably justified these withdrawals in part by Brodhead's inability to provision all that he had.

The unhappy colonel complained to the president of Congress, Samuel Huntington, that he was being neglected. To Washington he sarcastically referred to Clark's "supposed unbounded influence" with the westerners, and he protested vigorously against giving up Gibson's regiment to Clark. He put as many obstacles as he could in the way of Captain Isaac Craig's artillery company designated for Clark.

Washington gave Brodhead what comfort he could. Repeating that Clark's campaign was "an enterprise of the highest importance to the peace and safety of the whole western frontier," which would shield Fort Pitt as well as other areas, the general nonetheless confirmed that he did not intend to approve Colonel Gibson's participation nor that of more than a company or two of his regiment, if Brodhead could spare them. He appeased the colonel by telling him that except for the lack of means to strengthen him, Brodhead would have been given command of the campaign.

Brodhead predicted Clark's failure and maliciously drew attention to the severe difficulty Clark was having in raising men. Finally, in a move at least partially aimed at depriving Clark of the necessary volunteers from the upper Ohio, Brodhead organized an attack against the Delawares. Gibson pointed out that men so engaged would not be willing to serve again and that many went on Brodhead's brief foray to avoid enlistment with Clark.

Crossing the Ohio in early April with three hundred men, Brodhead struck at the Delaware base, Coshocton. Marching through a heavy rain to surprise the town, he burned it, took thirty-five prisoners, and carried off a fortune in plunder. Of the captives, the fifteen men were bound and killed. The women and children, along with some friendly Moravian Christian Delawares found in the town, were taken to Pittsburgh. Brodhead had extreme difficulty restraining his men from killing the Christian Indians. As it was, on the return march warriors were encountered who asked to treat. Their distinguished-looking chief was promised safety and entered Brodhead's camp to talk. While he conferred with the colonel, an Indian-hating soldier stole up behind the chief and buried a tomahawk in his head.

Brodhead returned to find real trouble awaiting him at Fort Pitt. The auditor for the Western Department had reported misapplication of public funds to General Washington. Brodhead and his deputy quartermaster were charged. A large number of people in the vicinity had signed a long list of complaints against the colonel, some of his officers accused him, and the president of Pennsylvania contended that adequate supplies had been furnished Fort Pitt which the commander must have misused.

On 6 May Brodhead turned over his command to Colonel Gibson and returned to Philadelphia to be arraigned. Now only Clark remained to carry the hopes of the frontier.

Late in March Clark was still at Stewart's Crossing on the Youghiogheny endeavoring to raise men. Brodhead's constant quibbling delayed his efforts, as did Tory activity, and persistent attacks by the Indians along the upper Ohio and back into Westmoreland County. These factors discouraged men from engaging to leave their homes.

Depressing word came from Fort Jefferson. Captain George had been furnished poorly preserved meat. "Although the meat does not absolutely stink," George wrote, it came close to it. He had used up all his liquor supply to pay Indians to hunt game for the garrison. Only part of a song Clark had written and sent to him provided Captain George with any merriment!

Like Brodhead, Clark was tasting failure. "My situation is truly disagreeable," he wrote to Jefferson. He had struggled for so long to fight a war with inadequate means that "there is an indignity in it that often hurt me."

But the frustrations of Brodhead and Clark were no strangers to commanders in the East. From Washington on down leaders faced the lack of money, men, and supplies that forced them to inactivity. It is not surprising in such a lengthy struggle that leaders confronted flagging zeal.

Twelve

The West Hangs in the Balance

Late in June 1781, already running about three months behind schedule, Clark prepared to start down the Ohio. His efforts to supply the expedition had been successful. He had boats, artillery, and provisions for two thousand men—enough to leave a substantial amount of flour to ease the shortage at Fort Pitt. After a grand barbecue and ball given by Colonel Gibson, Clark moved his force of four hundred down-river to Wheeling. Here he paused, awaiting the arrival of Colonel Archibald Lochry, the Westmoreland leader. Alone among the Pennsylvania militia commanders, Lochry had constantly tried to cooperate with the Continental and Virginia contingents in the upper Ohio region. Although Clark could persuade very few Pennsylvanians to enlist with him, Lochry had promised to join him with a small volunteer force of about one hundred.

Too often disappointed in his expectations, Clark prepared to move on without Lochry on 7 August. The longer he waited, the more men deserted. Further delay would put his whole project in danger. Lochry arrived a day after Clark's departure. Sending word ahead that he was almost without provisions, Lochry started after the main body. Clark at once detached eight men under Captain Wallace to wait at an island with provisions. He also detailed Major Cracraft to remain with a small guard to provide Lochry with a large boat for the horses. The Pennsylvanians had been slowed by the necessity of bringing their horses along the shore.

On 16 August Lochry reached this group, loaded his horses aboard, and sent another party ahead to inform Clark of his progress. Unknown to Clark or Lochry, the celebrated Iroquois chief, Joseph Brant, had arrived on the Ohio in support of the British rangers and their Indians. Brant, with a hundred warriors, intercepted Lochry's messengers, learned of his plans, and lay in wait for the Pennsylvania men.

On 24 August Lochry landed his men to cook provisions and cut forage for the horses at a point about ten miles below the mouth of the Miami near a small creek that flowed into the Ohio (now called Laughery Creek, near what is now Aurora, Indiana). Here Brant's war party fell upon Lochry's force, killing about a third of the men and capturing the rest. Lochry was among the dead.

Brant then joined with four hundred rangers and Indians moving down the Ohio under Captain Andrew Thompson and the partisan leader, Alexander McKee. They followed the unsuspecting Clark to within twenty-five miles of the Falls. There the Indians refused to attempt an attack. But persuaded that Clark was not strong enough to try an invasion, they split into small bands, most returning to their villages. The rangers, short on food, retreated to Detroit.

Faced with wholesale desertions and a threat of mutiny, Clark had been unable to wait for Lochry. He was lucky. His army was the objective of Brant, Thompson, and McKee. Had the Lochry ambush not delayed Brant's rendezvous with the others, the combined force of over five hundred might have caught Clark at a serious disadvantage while the Americans were still on the river.

§ Clark Disappointed Again

The loss of Lochry's company was a blow to Clark's hopes. He smarted at the blame bitter Pennsylvanians laid on him for not protecting Lochry's advance. More bad news awaited him at Louisville. Governor Jefferson had resigned on 3 June, 1781, under fire for his conduct of the war. Shortly thereafter the Virginia legislature directed the new governor, Thomas Nelson, to cancel the Detroit expedition. Moreover, the troops expected from the inner counties had not been able to gather, tied down by Tory activity and the marauding Cherokee and Creeks.

Clark's preparations had spared the Kentucky stations from major attack during the summer. But many people had moved away to escape military service, enormous quantities of meat stored for the campaign had spoiled, and the chronic shortage of money, credit, and food was everywhere evident. Kentucky had lost almost fifty men killed by Indians in the first four months of the year, including Clark's reliable former officer, William Linn. John Floyd, the veteran surveyor, reported a successful hunt during the winter in which he had bagged fifty-four buffalo, four elk, and two wild hogs. Unfortunately his boat sank in a windstorm and he lost the meat as well as all the land surveys he had made over seven years' time. The indefatigable woodsman wryly reported, "This is my second defeat at sea, but I am yet alive and hearty." (Floyd had engaged in a brief fling as a privateer, was captured, and spent time in a British prison.)

The effort to maintain Fort Jefferson at the mouth of the Ohio had failed. After months while "the savages are constantly pecking at us," the fort was without everything. It was abandoned by early fall 1781. But Colonel Slaughter had completed a strong fort at Louisville, named Fort Nelson for the new governor of Virginia. Even this brought Clark

Thomas Nelson, Jr. (1738-1789), governor of
Virginia, June 1781 to November 1781. Nelson
is shown here as a youth in his only known
portrait. Portly and asthmatic, he retired from
the governorship for reasons of health after
only six months.

From the collection of the Virginia Museum of Fine Arts,
Richmond, Virginia.

criticism for being too far down the Ohio to be effective in guarding the crossings farther up used by the Indians in their attacks on the Kentucky River settlements.

Clark still planned some move against the enemy. Though many thought his strength sufficient only to guard Kentucky, the Ohio, and crucial storehouses of weapons and provisions, he scheduled an attack against the Indians on the Miami for September, coordinated with a strike by Colonel Gibson from Fort Pitt against the Wyandots in the Sandusky region. Clark expected this would be his last effort. With the end of the season's campaigning weather, Clark would probably lose his special general's commission. Further, rumors filtered west that the peacemakers in Europe were nearing an agreement to end the war.

Even this campaign failed to develop. Colonel Brodhead had resumed command at Fort Pitt while he awaited trial on the charges against him. He would not release Gibson for an attack and the disaffected troops around Pittsburgh would not serve on an expedition led by the discredited Brodhead. When Washington finally ordered Brodhead to give up the command on 17 September, it was too late for Gibson to support Clark's plan.

Weakened by additional desertions and discouraged, Clark left it to a conference of Kentucky militia leaders at Louisville to decide what to do. The most cautious, John Todd and Benjamin Logan, recommended a new fort at the mouth of the Kentucky. A few were willing to try another raid against the Shawnee, but Clark decided it was not worth the effort.

The weary and disheartened Clark settled down at Fort Nelson for the winter. He agreed to keep the little garrison at Vincennes at least through the winter but estimated that America had lost the interest of at least two-thirds of the Indians he had once won. Altogether, he gloomily concluded, "I have lost the object that was one of the principal inducements to my fatigues and transactions for several years past—my chain appears to have run out."

§ **War in the East Winds Down**

The outcome of this year of war was not so bad as Clark thought. His efforts had forestalled a major British campaign in the West. Faith in Clark had kept alive sufficient hope to prevent any serious decline in settlement. His vigor and leadership had accomplished far more than anyone could have imagined, considering the obstacles he had to overcome and the general condition of both the frontier and the equally strained seaboard. Clark would soon learn that the British had left the South and that Cornwallis, pinned down at Yorktown, would surrender his army on 19 October, 1781, to the combined French and American forces. The fighting was almost over in the original states. But the West still faced another bloody year of Indian warfare in 1782.

While Clark had struggled to organize his campaign in the early months of 1781, the Spanish on the upper Mississippi launched an attack of their own against the battered little British post at St. Joseph. In January, Captain Eugenio Pourré went against the almost defenseless position with about sixty men from St. Louis and Cahokia accompanied by about the same number of Indians. Governor Francisco Cruzat at St. Louis probably authorized the raid to satisfy some Milwaukee chiefs who wanted plunder. He may have thought it would also serve to discourage another British attack on St. Louis as well as offering an opportunity to revenge de la Balme's defeat. The Potawatomi who might have helped the British defend the fort were bought off by a promise of some of the loot. St. Joseph surrendered promptly; Pourré stayed only a day, proclaiming the territory won in the name of Spain. The Spanish government used this to claim a portion of the region east of the Mississippi.

§ War in the West Continues

General William Irvine, ordered to take command at Fort Pitt in November 1781, slowly restored the confidence of that area. The same month Benjamin Harrison, long-time leader of the Virginia House, replaced Nelson as the state's governor. Nelson had retired because of failing health.

During the following year (1782) Harrison had to contend with a disastrous decline of the situation in the West. With the surrender of Cornwallis, the fighting in the East had virtually ended. But neither the British nor the Americans were willing to accept stalemate west of the mountains. As leading frontiersmen pointed out to Harrison, the fate of the West hung in the balance.

Harrison followed his predecessors in supporting Clark's policies despite doubts about the commander raised by a number of protests. These protests originated with Clark's rivals and other dissidents. The strain of unceasing warfare, hardship, and constant danger showed itself increasingly in the quarrels, recriminations, exaggerated fears and rash actions of this last year of the war. Harrison might have helped the borderers more by extending Virginia's support to Irvine at Fort Pitt, whose position covered the exposed stations of eastern Kentucky more effectively than Clark's did at Fort Nelson. But by early 1782 Virginia had again exhausted its resources. In January the governor reported only one shilling in the treasury and in April admitted that the westerners must make their own provisions for defense—"we have but four shillings in the Treasury and no means of getting any more." Neither he nor the Congress could help Irvine; the most stringent economies were enjoined on Clark and his officers.

Clark's outlook as the year opened was clearly divided. With the end of the war in sight, he wanted time to concern himself with land acquisitions for himself and his family. He was offended by a legislative commission sent to look into the snarled financial accounts of his command. He asked to resign. Harrison quickly assured Clark the investigation was not aimed at him and expressed complete confidence in him, renewing his commission as general and approving Clark's plans to build additional forts on the Ohio and to provide armed boats to patrol the river. The general was one "whose character has ever stood unimpeached," he wrote.

Clark accepted the challenge willingly. He was sure that war with the Indians would continue even when British-led attacks ended. He expected the year would bring "greater dangers than I have heretofore—there is no knowing the fate

General William Irvine, M.D. (1741-1804), painted by James R. Lambdin (1807-1889). General Irvine was commander at Fort Pitt from November 1781 to the end of the American Revolution. He was born in Ireland of Scots ancestry. He settled at Carlisle, Pennsylvania, about 1764.

Courtesy of the New-York Historical Society, New York City.

of war." On the one hand, he was discouraged, fearing "it will be out of my power to save this infant country from those impending strokes that now hover over it," but on the other hand, he thought the outcome would be known by the end of the summer. If it was successful, he looked forward eagerly to a time when he would live peacefully in the new lands with his father and brothers settled nearby.

§ **The Gnadenhutten Massacre**

The cruel warfare of 1782 opened in March when Colonel David Williamson led three hundred men from western Pennsylvania and the Monongahela against the peaceful Christian Delawares at Gnadenhutten on the Muskingum River. Williamson suspected that the village had been taken over by hostile Delawares with the British. He found over ninety defenseless men, women, and children. After staying with them peacefully for three days, the frontiersmen cold-bloodedly bound and slaughtered the entire population.

This "Gnadenhutten Massacre" ensured the fate of another expedition in the early summer. Colonel William Crawford had narrowly won election over the popular Williamson for command of the Pittsburgh militia. With five hundred men, he led an attack on the Indian towns of the Sandusky River. Smarting for revenge, five hundred Mingo, Wyandot, Munsee, and Delaware warriors met Crawford's force in the open along the upper Sandusky. The once-friendly Captain Pipe had the support of British rangers under Captain William Caldwell and the notorious Simon Girty. Only about one hundred of Crawford's men were experienced fighters. After an initial stand, the Americans broke into disorderly retreat when a band of Shawnee arrived to reinforce Pipe. Williamson restored some order but Crawford was missing and fifty had been killed or captured.

The most fortunate of the captured were taken to Sandusky and tomahawked. The Indians reserved a crueler fate for the captured commander. In revenge for Gnadenhutten, they stripped Crawford and tied him to a stake over red-hot coals, poked and beat him with burning sticks, and scalped him alive. After two hours, he begged the amused Simon Girty to shoot him and end his suffering. When Crawford fell into the fire, squaws shoveled the coals over him and his exposed skull. Only Dr. John Knight, taken with Crawford, escaped to tell the story. Crawford had died bravely, in silence.

§ **Defeat at Blue Licks**

Farther south, Indians began to appear in numbers around the Kentucky stations in August. They were the forerunners of a massive British-led invasion directed against both Fort Pitt and Fort Nelson. Smaller parties had been active on the upper Ohio and in Kentucky since February; in July Indians had destroyed Hannastown, thirty-five miles east of Pittsburgh. They also killed or captured twenty-five at another nearby village. The Pennsylvanians wanted to kill Indians and take land, according to General Irvine, but they would not send men to support any offensive he suggested.

The appearance of the first of Clark's gunboats on the

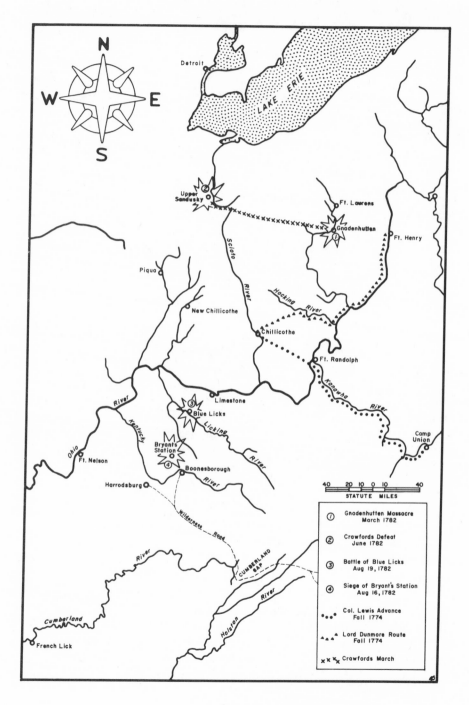

War in the Ohio Valley, 1774-1782.

Ohio, armored and mounting small cannon, may have diverted an attack on Wheeling. At the end of July, in a final effort to keep possession of the West, the British sent Captain William Caldwell, Alexander McKee, Matthew Elliott, and Simon and George Girty with over a thousand rangers and Indians down the Miami to the Ohio crossings. Too fearful to attack Louisville where Clark was, or the garrisons at Wheeling and Fort Pitt, many lingered along the river keeping an eye on the gunboat.

Three or four hundred descended on Bryan's Station, where militia were already gathering for defense. On 16 August, 1782, from sunrise until ten the next morning, Bryan's withstood the siege. The fort was without water when the first sign of Indians appeared. In a daring ruse, all the women at the post walked calmly to a nearby spring, filled every available container with water, and returned safely. The Indians, seeking surprise, let them pass. The forty or so men declined to be drawn out of the fort, putting up a fierce fight. Reinforcements from Lexington fell into an ambush and had to retreat, although seventeen mounted men dashed for the fort and made it.

By noon the next day the Indians were gone. Men from Lexington, Harrodsburg, and Boonesborough arrived and promptly went in pursuit. A large party under Colonel Benjamin Logan was expected, but the men gathered under Colonels John Todd, Stephen Trigg, and Daniel Boone would not wait.

The Indians retreated slowly, hoping to draw pursuit. Boone was suspicious because they left such a clear trail. The Kentuckians, about two hundred in number, caught up with them about forty miles to the east at the lower Blue Licks. Boone, who had accurately estimated the size of the enemy, urged delay until Logan's men arrived. The other leaders appeared indecisive but impulsively followed Major Hugh McGary into the ravines along the Licking. Boone, on the left, was drawn ahead by the wily warriors while Indians attacked from ambush in front and behind the companies of Todd and Trigg.

Within five minutes the attack became a rout, with the militia fleeing for their lives. Some of the most prominent men in Kentucky fell in this Battle of the Blue Licks on 19 August, 1782, including John Todd, Stephen Trigg, and Boone's son, Israel. An estimated sixty or seventy were left on the field. The rest straggled back to their stations or to Bryan's, passing through Logan's column marching up in support.

Logan, with nearly five hundred men, lost no time in returning to the Licks. The Indians had gone. The colonel contented himself with burying the dead. He returned hastily to guard the settlements for fear the powerful British-led force would strike again. Some suggested he might have gone after them, but Benjamin Logan had always been a cautious man, if not the "dull, narrow body from whom nothing clever need be expected," as he was called by the critical veteran, Colonel Arthur Campbell.

It was the last major British attack below the Ohio. But the settlers could not know this. Grief affected everyone and panic struck many. Boone, survivor of many close calls, remained throughout his life most moved by this encounter. Soon afterward he lamented, "We can scarcely behold a spot of earth but what reminds us of the fall of some fellow adventurer massacred by savage hands. Our number of militia [is] decreased. Our widows and orphans are numerous. Our officers and worthiest men fall a sacrifice."

Recriminations flew back and forth. Leaders at the Kentucky River stations were critical of Clark and complained to Governor Harrison, who had approved Clark's policies. The forts at the mouths of the Kentucky and Licking rivers and at Limestone Creek had not been built. Clark had lavished his attention on Fort Nelson and on the project for armed boats. The latter had produced only one, so far, and even if there were more it was an easy matter for Indians to evade their patrols. Boone put it bluntly when he criticized the Virginia government's support of Clark and neglect of the rest of Kentucky. He referred to "Louisville, a town without inhabitants, a fort situated in such a manner that the enemy coming with a design to lay waste our country would scarcely come within one hundred miles of it."

§ Clark Rebuked

Harrison expressed startled surprise that the forts he had ordered had not been built. In a sharp rebuke to Clark he wrote, "I expect implicit obedience . . . and will not again overlook a breach of duty." The next day he wrote again, in a milder tone, complaining that he had received no reports from the commander for several months. Harrison wanted an explanation of the failure to construct additional forts, reprovingly adding, "It gives me great pain to find that you have disappointed us in our expectations."

His letters crossed those of Clark, who expressed a strong opinion that the tragedy had been caused by the "reprehensible conduct" of the leaders at Blue Licks who had been so entirely lacking in prudence. Colonel Crockett, to whom the governor had addressed inquiries, testified handsomely to Clark's conduct. Clark, he told the governor, had "strained every nerve in his power" to achieve results, adding an enumeration of the difficulties the general labored under.

When Harrison's letters came, Clark, stung by the governor's accusations, put the problems on the line. He pointed out that sending additional dispatches would cost money. Enemy activity had prevented work on the new forts. The stations had refused to provide men, money, or tools. In fact, the very leaders who now complained had advised Clark to postpone construction. Even if the forts had been built, the frontier had neither men nor provisions to stock them.

Clark was reluctant to criticize his old friend, John Todd. But it was true, Clark told Harrison, that Todd, who had died at the Licks, had been released with his company from other duty to maintain a network of scouts to warn of attack. Clearly Todd had failed.

Clark directed Harrison's attention to the fact that those critics to whom Harrison had listened were part of the "new state" faction seeking secession from Virginia. Clark and his friends, loyal to their state, had made enemies of that group. Then, subtly shifting responsibility to the state, Clark noted that he was now selling his own land to raise the money

Benjamin Harrison (1726-1791), governor of Virginia, 1781 to 1784. He was the fifth of that name, a signer of the Declaration of Independence, and father of President William Henry Harrison.

Courtesy of the President Benjamin Harrison Foundation, Indianapolis.

to keep his one post, Fort Nelson, strong. Clearly, if more was required it would be up to the state to find the means.

§ Clark Moves Against Indians

Meanwhile, the Blue Licks defeat called for retaliation. Clark was bent on one more thrust against the Indians before the war ended and his longed-for retirement was granted. He planned another march against the Shawnee in cooperation with an attack by General Irvine against the Wyandots and Delawares. Irvine's part was canceled by orders from Congress's Board of War. The Board was ordering a cessation of hostilities after hearing the welcome news that peace preliminaries had been signed. Irvine did not disclose the change in order to hold the Indians who had been his target from reinforcing those Clark was moving against.

Over one thousand men crossed the Ohio at the Licking on 3 November, 1782. The Shawnee fled from Chillicothe. Clark's advance guard killed a few and took some prisoners, but most of the Indians escaped. Detachments fanned out to destroy five towns, along with their crops—Colonel Logan with one hundred fifty horsemen went all the way to Miamistown, which he burned. After waiting a few days, hoping for a fight, Clark retired to the Ohio by 18 November.

The testy governor reproved Clark for not consulting him before going on the raid. It seemed an unnecessary campaign in view of the fact that the British were calling in their warriors. But everyone on the frontier knew that although the war with Britain might be over, the struggle with the Indians would go on. Harrison soon realized that such a fall attack, destroying the Indians' crops, had been a timely stroke and congratulated Clark on his success, acknowledging his "spirited and judicious conduct," and the "highest sense of the important service you have rendered." The contrite governor tried to explain that if Clark had objections to anything he had said, he had only to keep the governor more fully informed to avoid criticism.

Harrison now assured Clark that he would be permitted to resign in the spring. A reduction in officers for the sake of economy made a general unnecessary in the Kentucky establishment.

Clark remained at Fort Nelson through the winter, helping the western commissioners unsnarl the soldiers' pay accounts and those of the army's suppliers. He gave thought to what would be needed in the year to come if the Indians remained hostile—as they did for many years—or if the British went back on the cease-fire. In May he returned to Richmond. Still unpaid for his long service, he wrote in embarrassment to ask the governor for a personal loan to buy clothes! All he had received from Virginia, himself, was the award of a sword, and a secondhand one at that.

On 2 July, 1783, Harrison relieved Clark of his command, with effusive thanks and generous praise. The governor noted that Virginia had no money; it could afford no further expedition against the Indians. Harrison agreed with Clark that the Indians should be forced, not begged, to ask for peace, but more warfare was impossible. Consequently, Virginia had no need for a general in the West. Clark graciously thanked the governor and promised his services for the future whenever they might be needed.

Clark had learned in April that the terms of the peace gave the United States all the land he had fought for. Some states were insisting that the lands west of the mountains should become the property of the whole United States. They refused to ratify the new government of the Articles of Confederation until the states with western lands gave them up. But Virginia was still insisting upon its western claims. Those who had fought loyally for the Old Dominion from the Forks of the Ohio to its mouth and beyond to the Mississippi could not know of the many new states that would one day spread across the lands on which they had struggled.

Thirteen

The Peacemakers and the West

Historians have long argued whether or not the military actions in the West won it for the new United States. The last years of the war indicate a military stand-off. At the end, neither side had prevailed. The British could only hit and run below the Ohio, nor could General Irvine at Fort Pitt or General Clark on the lower Ohio, do more north of the river. Weak as the Americans were, strung out in their forts and settlements, the British were no stronger. Their Regulars were few, sickness pervaded the ranks of the rangers, the French were lukewarm or openly disloyal and the Indians were wavering and undependable, demanding ever more lavish supplies and presents.

Farther west, the British had lost the Mississippi and Wabash forts but the Americans, having won them, had not been able to maintain them. The principal ones, Vincennes, Kaskaskia, and Cahokia, had reverted to the care of the mistreated French, who held them insecurely and grudgingly for Virginia. The fact remains, they did hold them, as well as a tenuous control over the Indians in those areas. At the end, J. M. P. Le Gras at Vincennes still considered himself commander in the pay of Virginia as did Timothé de Monbreun at Kaskaskia.

Whatever the military situation was, a great deal of responsibility rested on the diplomats. They could give up what Americans thought had been won. British peacemakers had twice done just that, to the utter despair of the American colonists during the earlier colonial wars.

Much depended on the personalities and forcefulness of the American peace commissioners, Benjamin Franklin, John Adams, and John Jay. It remained to be seen whether Congress, the author of their instructions, could or even would try to hold the West in the peace treaty.

The outcome was dependent, too, on the demands of the other belligerents, Britain, France, and Spain, and to some extent on the opinions of Russia and Austria, to whom the warring powers looked for possible mediation. Further, since the negotiations took place over an extended period while the war went on, the changing military situation tended to determine how much each participant demanded on any particular date.

The original instructions of the Continental Congress to the peace commissioners (14 August, 1779) advised them to claim the area of the West from Canada to Florida and west to the Mississippi. Congress knew of Clark's conquests in the Illinois country, as did Franklin in Paris, before the end of 1779. How much this achievement weighed in the thinking of the peace commissioners is unknown.

By the summer of 1781 the French envoy, La Luzerne, had established a dominant position with many American leaders. A large number of men in Congress appeared subservient to French policy. New instructions to the commissioners sought to bind them to whatever terms France should propose. Congress, over the objections of Virginia delegates, appeared to have receded from an absolute insistence on gaining the West. La Luzerne won a further victory in the election of Robert R. Livingston as new Secretary for Foreign Affairs. Inexperienced and lazy, Livingston was even more pro-French than Congress.

France was prepared to sacrifice America's interests. It was desperate to get out of the war. France's finances were shattered. By the fall of 1782, France was ready to give every-thing north of the Ohio to Britain, leaving Kentucky to the Americans, and putting Spain over the lands south of the Cumberland River.

Spain, meanwhile, asserted its demands for everything west of a line running roughly north and south from the western end of Lake Erie.

Benjamin Franklin was inclined to follow orders, accepting French direction of the peace effort in the expectation that France would hold out for a treaty giving the West to the United States. Though he appeared more confident of the good intentions of France than Adams and Jay, he was not, in reality, prepared to give up the West. John Adams had always been suspicious of French policy; Jay was even more so. When the latter two found out that France was negotiating with Britain behind their backs, they became convinced that France did not merit the trust of Congress. Therefore they determined not to be bound by their instructions. They convinced Franklin that the French policy, which in turn was influenced by France's ally, Spain, would be disastrous to the American cause.

They were right. France was, in fact, so anxious to end the war that it was considering a cease-fire that would not even guarantee British withdrawal from the territory of the original thirteen states, let alone assure American independence. La Luzerne even intimated as much to the Congress.

In face of George III's opposition to granting independence and Spain's demand for Gibraltar as a requisite for peace, France, to end the war, had to think of other terms to offer Britain and other territory, such as the American West, that might compensate Spain for the failure to get Gibraltar.

Convinced of French perfidy, the American negotiators turned to direct talks with British representatives. They flatly disobeyed the instructions of Congress. Britain, in turn, was inclined to be generous after many tedious changes of policy. A new prime minister, Lord Shelburne, saw that a liberal policy might restore Britain's trade with its former colonies even if government of them was lost. It would help to drive a wedge between the United States and France, Britain's enemy. In addition, by awarding generous boundaries to the new nation Shelburne was showing a realistic desire to avert future friction as Americans inevitably moved west.

But Shelburne's generosity had its limits, as did the terms he would have to justify to Parliament. France wanted to keep the new country small and weak. Spain had no wish for close neighbors along the Mississippi. Only Jay's forceful insistence on the Mississippi boundary, ably seconded by Adams and Franklin, ensured that the West would go to the United States.

The American representatives signed the preliminary treaty with Britain on 30 November, 1782. Though they had violated their instructions, to have done otherwise would not have been in the best interests of the United States. Wisely, they had ignored the mandate of the weak, French-dominated Congress. Strictly speaking, they had not broken the treaty with France forbidding a separate peace insofar as the terms agreed upon with the British were not to take effect until France had completed agreements with Britain on other matters. The full Treaty of Paris was signed 3 September, 1783.

The fact that the American diplomats held out for a western boundary at the Mississippi reflects both the claims of certain states based on their colonial charters and, doubtless, the military efforts westerners had expended during the conflict. That Shelburne granted such terms indicates the general war-weariness of Britain, the demonstrated cost of trying to hold forts and Indians in the area, and the political considerations already mentioned.

Beyond all this, for the areas of the upper Ohio, of Kentucky, and of middle Tennessee the fact that increasing numbers of Americans moved into these regions, put down roots, and stayed, was probably the most important reason for the peacemakers to award them to the United States. Anything else would have been unrealistic and productive of future trouble from the aggressive frontiersmen.

Yet without those who marched and fought, suffered and died, even the most stubborn and undaunted families could not have remained. In Kentucky and farther west in the Illinois country, many proclaimed at the time that only their faith in George Rogers Clark kept them in the West. Even the Spanish sought his presence. Had Clark not procured Hamilton's surrender, that British commander might well have succeeded in driving all the Americans back east of the mountains. For Hamilton showed by his impetuous march down the Wabash to Vincennes that he and Clark were made of the same sort of stuff.

Thus, without the settlement and the intrepid fighting that preserved it—however small-scale and inconclusive it was, militarily—even John Jay could not have resisted efforts to deprive America of the West.

Only the Indians were forgotten in the peace treaty. All along the back country, from the Great Lakes to the Gulf, they would continue their depredations, trying hopelessly to preserve their homes from white encroachment. By war and by treaty, the United States would push them back, ever westward, until late in the nineteenth century when they were fragmented and confined to reservations, living on the government's meager bounty. Until then, unwary settlers on the frontier would feel their sting.

The lands the Big Knives had fought for became part of the public domain when states ceded their western claims to the United States—Virginia in 1784. Out of the area that figured so prominently in the Americans' war in the West during the Revolutionary period came eight new states: Kentucky in 1792, Tennessee in 1796, Ohio in 1803. Indiana became a state in 1816 and Illinois in 1818, when the end of the War of 1812 eliminated British influence over the Indians, encouraging more rapid settlement. Michigan achieved statehood in 1837, Wisconsin in 1848. West Virginia became a state only when it separated from Virginia during the Civil War.

Many of the states retained lands in the West as bounties for their war veterans. Virginia had voted lands in January 1781, for the men who went with Clark to the Illinois country; not the three hundred acres promised each officer and man by Jefferson, Mason, and Wythe when the Kaskaskia expedition was inaugurated, but a total of one hundred fifty thousand acres later divided proportionately by rank. In 1783 a board of commissioners was appointed to locate and survey the land, which was formally recognized as the Illinois or Clark Grant at the end of 1786. Located on the north side of the Ohio in the present Indiana counties of Scott, Floyd, and Clark, the lands were apportioned to those still alive, the heirs of the dead, and those to whom Clark's veterans had transferred their claims. The task occupied the commissioners, of whom Clark himself was one. To within a few years of his death, Clark served as chairman of the commission. The town of Clarksville, across from Louisville, was laid out in the southwestern corner of the grant and there Clark settled in a simple log house on a bluff overlooking the lower falls.

America's first and longest war had ended. The War for American Independence had a transforming effect on the nation's people. With independence came an elevation of spirit, a sense of enterprise and experimentation in every sphere of life. "Great things" had indeed been effected "by a few men well conducted."

Portrait from life of George Rogers Clark attributed to C. D. Cook, depicting Clark as embittered and ailing.

Courtesy of National Portrait Gallery, Smithsonian Institution, Washington, D.C.

Suggestions for Additional Reading

Original materials for this account are in the Draper Collection at the State Historical Society of Wisconsin, the Virginia State Archives, the Canadian Archives, the Library of Congress, and in public and private collections in many states. The most important are in two collections: *George Rogers Clark Papers*, volume 1, 1771-1781, volume 2, 1781-1784, edited by James Alton James (Springfield, Illinois, 1912 and 1926); and in the series, *Documentary History of Dunmore's War, 1774* (Madison, Wisconsin, 1905) *Revolution on the Upper Ohio, 1775-1777* (Madison, Wisconsin, 1908). *Frontier Defense on the Upper Ohio, 1777-1778* (Madison, Wisconsin, 1912), edited by Reuben Gold Thwaites and Louise Phelps Kellogg, and *Frontier Advance on the Upper Ohio, 1778-1779* (Madison, Wisconsin, 1916), *Frontier Retreat on the Upper Ohio, 1779-1781* (Madison, Wisconsin, 1917), edited by Louise Phelps Kellogg.

Documents, maps, portraits, and articles have been printed in magazines and journals of state and local historical societies both in the East and in the Midwest concerning various aspects of the American Revolution in the West and accounts of persons who were active in it.

A convenient summary of all the frontier areas is provided by Jack M. Sosin, *The Revolutionary Frontier 1763-1783* (New York, 1967), which includes an excellent bibliography of books and articles on specific aspects of the subject.

The most readable and reliable biographies of George Rogers Clark are James A. James, *The Life of George Rogers Clark* (Chicago, 1928) and John Bakeless, *Background to Glory: The Life of George Rogers Clark* (Philadelphia, 1957). For Daniel Boone see Bakeless, *Daniel Boone* (New York, 1939). John D. Barnhart has edited Lieutenant Governor Henry Hamilton's journal with a perceptive introduction in a scarce but valuable book, *Henry Hamilton and George Rogers Clark in the American Revolution* (Crawfordsville, Indiana, 1951).

A broad treatment of Revolutionary events on the frontier is Dale VanEvery, *A Company of Heroes* (New York, 1962). The southwestern settlement may be traced in Samuel Cole Williams, *Tennessee During the Revolutionary War* (Nashville, 1944), and in Harriette Simpson Arnow, *Seedtime on the Cumberland* (New York, 1960).

Index